D1372650

SOUTHERN STYLE

Tea Time

did someone say tea?

by

Rosemary Newman and Sharon Strickland

Authors of Southern Ladies Know How To Cook It

Copyright 2001

Library of Congress #2001116664

Dedication

to our granddaughters
Christa, Sydney, Sarah
and Cailey
for tea parties past and
the ones to come.

with love

Printed by Allied Printing
Published by Rosemary Newman and Sharon Strickland
Cover by Cottonpatch, Inc. and Avonne Beaver
Designed and Illustrated by Avonne Beaver
Photography by Doug Cotton and Gina Palmer

You are

cordially invited

to join us for tea...

Welcome
To Our Tea Party!

"There are many kinds of tea, but each one is special when shared by you and me."

1999 R. Newman

Two For Tea

When I saw this little book,
I had to stop and take a look
The title so fitting, *Two For Tea*
It brought back memories of you and me.
I remember two little girls playing dress up
in ribbons and lace,
Makeup smeared on each sweet little face.
Big floppy hats falling over our eyes,
You'd made play tea for us! Oh, what a surprise!
It was just plain water colored with dirt.
But that didn't matter, we admired your hard work.
The tea cakes were mud shaped so neat,
They were absolutely delicious, we pretended to eat.
Time went by too quickly, we were soon grown.
With houses and families to care for of our own.
But memories live forever and it's a fact,
To recall something so precious, one just has to think back.
In my mind's eye I can see, two little girls preparing to tea.
I can see you and I can see me.

- 1998 Sharon Strickland

Favorite Tea Time Photos

Regular Iced Tea

1 quart of water in saucepan
4 small tea bags (your choice)

Let water come to a boil and reduce heat to low. Place tea bags into water and allow to steep for 10 minutes. Add 1/2 cup sugar and stir. Yield: 1 quart.
Note: this recipe may be served hot or cold. If served hot, add rock candy to replace sugar.

Peach Tea

1/2 gallon of water
6 tea bags
1 cup sugar
2 tablespoons peach extract

Bring 1 quart of water to boil. Turn heat to low and add tea bags. Steep for ten minutes; add sugar and stir. Add peach extract and add enough water to make 1/2 gallon. Pour over ice to cool. Garnish with peach slices.

"*Tea makes me happy.*"

1999 R. Newman

Cinnamon Tea

1 quart of water
8 tea bags or 1 cup loose tea
1 1/2 cups sugar
2 tablespoons cinnamon - cinnamon sticks
1 lemon

Bring water to boil in saucepan. Add tea bags or loose tea; steep for ten minutes. Take tea bags out or drain tea. Add sugar and stir. Add 2 tablespoons of cinnamon; add water to make 1 gallon. Heat on medium until first boil. Place cinnamon stick in each cup accompanied with a lemon wedge.

Lemon Tea

1 gallon of water
8 tea bags
1 1/2 cups sugar
Lemon wedges or slices

Bring to boil in saucepan, 1 quart of water. Lower heat; add tea bags. Let steep. Add sugar and pour over ice. Place lemon on lip of glass. Add water to make one gallon.

Hot Orange Tea

1 gallon of water
8 tea bags, regular or orange flavored
1 1/2 cups sugar
1 orange wedge

Bring to boil in saucepan, 1 quart of water. Lower heat and steep tea bags with orange wedge for 10 minutes. Add sugar and stir; add remaining water. Place orange slices on glass for garnish.

Tea says, "I'm sorry."

Sparkling Tea Punch

2 quarts boiling water
2 sticks cinnamon
20 whole cloves
2/3 cup loose tea
1 cup sugar
32 ounces frozen lemonade
4 cups water
2 quarts ginger ale
2 (No. 2) cans pineapple juice

Add cinnamon and cloves to boiling water. Remove from heat and add tea. Brew 4 minutes, uncovered; strain. Add remaining ingredients and blend well. Place block of ice in punch bowl and pour mixture over ice. Chill. Stir and serve. Makes 25 to 30 punch cup servings.

Instant Russian Tea

2 cups instant orange drink (i.e. tang)
1 cup sugar
1/2 cup instant tea
1 teaspoon ground cinnamon
1/2 teaspoon ground cloves

Mix ingredients well. Makes one quart of dry ingredients. Use 2 heaping teaspoons to one cup water. Yield: 1 quart dry ingredients.

"Life is like a peach.
Sometimes a little fuzzy
on the outside but so
sweet on the inside."

R. Newman

Mint Green Tea

1 quart of water
4 bags of green tea or 1/2 cup loose green tea
1/2 cup sugar
Mint leaves

Boil water and reduce heat; add tea bags and steep for 10 minutes. Add sugar and pour over ice. Garnish with mint leaves.

Hot Spiced Tea

1 teaspoon whole cloves
1 stick cinnamon
2 quarts cold water
1 1/4 cups sugar
4 small tea bags
Juice of 3 oranges
Juice of 1 1/2 lemons
1 (46-ounce) can pineapple juice
2 drops of red food coloring

Place sugar and spices (tied loosely in cloth) in water and bring to boil. Add tea bags. Allow to stand for ten minutes. Remove tea bags and spices. Add fruit juices. Let set overnight and heat to serve. Yield: 25 cups.

"*Tea is something shared often in a life time.*"

Johnny Appleseed Tea

2 quarts water
6 tea bags
6 ounces frozen apple juice
1/4 cup plus 2 teaspoons brown sugar

Boil one quart water and steep tea 5 minutes. Add other ingredients and 1 quart water and simmer over low heat until thoroughly heated.

Iced Red Zinger Tea

1 quart water
3 tea bags
1 quart cranberry juice
1/2 lemon
1 1/2 cups sugar

Pour quart of water into medium saucepan. Add 1 quart of cranberry juice; sugar and stir. Pour over ice. Add lemon slices on lip of glass.

Cranberry Tea

2 cups pineapple juice
2 cups cranberry juice cocktail
3 tea bags
1 3/4 cups water
1/2 cup brown sugar
2 cinnamon sticks
1 teaspoon cloves

Mix all ingredients in a coffee pot and perk for 10 minutes.

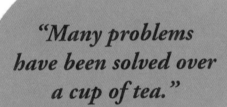

"*Many problems have been solved over a cup of tea.*"

S. Strickland

Lime &
Cottage Cheese Mold

Cucumber Sandwiches

Tea Cakes

Crystal Grapes

Tea For Two

served
with **Regular Iced Tea**

Lime and Cottage Cheese Mold

1 can (1 pound, 4 ounces)
  crushed pineapple
1/2 cup lemon juice
Boiling water
1 cup finely chopped celery
2 packages lime-flavored
  gelatin

1 cup chopped walnuts
2 tablespoons grated lemon rind
2 cups cottage cheese
  (1 pound)
1 teaspoon prepared
  horseradish
1/2 teaspoon salt

Drain syrup from pineapple into 4 cup measure and save for next step. Add lemon juice and enough boiling water to make 3 cups liquid; add gelatin and stir until dissolved; chill mixture until syrupy.

Spoon about 1 1/2 cups syrupy gelatin into a medium-sized bowl; fold in drained pineapple, walnuts and grated lemon rind; pour into lightly greased loaf pan, 9" x 5" x 3"; chill until just firm. Keep remaining syrupy gelation at room temperature. When layer in mold is firm; beat syrupy gelatin until fluffy; blend in cottage cheese, celery, horseradish and salt; spoon over layer in pan; chill until firm. Unmold onto serving plate; garnish with avocado slices, if you wish.

Cucumber Sandwiches

8 slices of bread, crust removed
2 cucumbers
1 (3 ounce) package cream cheese, room temperature
Dash of cayenne pepper
2 green onions and blades, chopped
1 tablespoon of mayonnaise

Slice cucumbers lengthwise; set aside. Cream together cream cheese and mayonnaise; add pepper; fold in onions and blades.

Spread on each slice of bread (prevents absorption of cucumber juice). Place layer of cucumber slices. Salt to taste. Cut into quarters.

Tea Cakes

1 egg	1 teaspoon baking soda
1 cup sugar	1/4 teaspoon baking powder
1/2 cup shortening	3 cups flour
1/2 cup buttermilk	1/8 teaspoon salt

Cream shortening and sugar until light and fluffy; add egg and beat well. Add soda to buttermilk and mix until it foams and add to egg mixture. Sift together flour, salt, and baking powder, and add to other ingredients to form a dough stiff enough to handle. Roll on lightly floured board to about 1/8 inch thickness. Cut with cookie cutter and place on baking sheet. Bake in 350 degree oven for about 10 minutes or until lightly browned. Yield: 5 or 6 dozen. (Extras can be frozen for future use.)

Crystal Grapes

1/2 pound red seedless grapes
1 egg white
1 cup granulated sugar

Rinse grapes leaving wet. Dig into egg white. Place sugar inside sturdy bag. Drop wet grapes in a few at a time. Shake until covered well. Place on cookie sheet in a single layer. Freeze until ready to use.

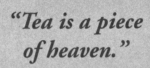

*"Tea is a piece
of heaven."*

R. Newman

Whole Wheat Sandwiches
with Cucumber, Crabmeat &
Sour Cream Filling

Horn of Plenty with
Chicken Salad on Lettuce

Peaches & Cream Shortcake
with Lite Whipped Cream

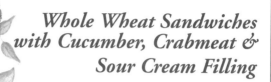

a savannah

Tea For Four

served
with **Peach Tea**

Whole Wheat Sandwiches with Cucumber, Crabmeat and Sour Cream Filling

1 cup crabmeat, cooked
1/3 cup peeled grated cucumbers
2 teaspoons minced chives
2 teaspoons fresh lemon juice
1/4 teaspoon salt
1/8 teaspoon dill
1/4 cup sour cream

Press moisture from cucumbers with paper towels. Combine all ingredients in order listed; mix well. Spread on whole wheat sandwich bread, crust removed and slice into quarters.

Horn of Plenty with Chicken Salad on Lettuce

Make the horn by removing bread from inside of french loaf. Line inside crust shell with lettuce. Stuff crust with freshly made chicken salad. Garnish with colorful fresh vegetables. This also makes a beautiful centerpiece. Accompany with sesame crackers.

Peaches and Cream Shortcake with Lite Whipped Cream

1 fresh or frozen pound cake, thawed
1-2 pounds fresh peaches, peeled and sliced
1 cup sugar
Light whipped cream in can

Pour sugar over peaches and allow to set for an hour or more in order for juice to make. Spoon peaches and juice over sliced cake. Top with whipped cream. Serve immediately.

Gala Asparagus

Cucumber Salad

Sliced Orange Acapulco

a gala

Brunch For Six

served with Hot Orange Tea

Gala Asparagus

4 small green onions, including blades, chopped
2 cups fresh mushrooms, sliced
6 tablespoons butter
1/2 cup walnuts, toasted
1/2 teaspoon salt
2 cans asparagus, drained

Saute onions and the mushrooms in butter until tender. Add the walnuts and salt. Spoon over heated asparagus.

Cucumber Salad

1 large cucumber
4 green onions, finely sliced
1/4 cup dry white wine
1/2 teaspoon lemon juice
3 tablespoons olive oil
Salt and pepper to taste
1 teaspoon dried basil, crushed
1 large head of lettuce cut into 6 sections

Peel and thinly slice cucumber and onions. Place in a bowl along with the wine and lemon juice. Marinate for one hour. Combine rest of ingredients together except lettuce, blending well. Pour over lettuce and toss to coat. Add the cucumber and onion mixture and toss again.

Sliced Orange Acapulco

7 medium oranges
1/2 cup powdered sugar
Ground cinnamon

Peel and section oranges removing all white membranes. Arrange on a platter around serving bowl of sifted powdered sugar. Just before serving, sprinkle with the 1/2 cup sifted powdered sugar and the cinnamon.

Hot Cheese Toast

Marinated Tomatoes

Bourbon Balls

some like it hot

Tea For Eight

served with **Cinnamon Tea**

Hot Cheese Toast

8 slices bacon,
  fried and drained
1/3 cup mayonnaise
1 cup shredded Cheddar cheese
1 small onion, grated
1 egg, slightly beaten

Salt and pepper to taste
1/2 teaspoon Worcestershire
  sauce
8 slices white bread
Paprika

Trim the crust from bread and crumble bacon; set aside. Combine rest of ingredients in order listed, mixing well. Stir in the crumbled bacon. Spread the mixture on bread slices. Sprinkle with paprika. Place on a cookie sheet and bake at 350 degrees for fifteen minutes or until lightly brown.

Marinated Tomatoes

2 tablespoons salad oil
2 teaspoons vinegar
1/2 garlic clove, crushed

1/3 teaspoon salt
1/4 teaspoon thyme
6 peeled tomatoes,
  cut into wedges

Combine first five ingredients; mix well. Pour over tomato wedges. Refrigerate several hours before serving. Drain excess liquid before serving or add shredded lettuce and use liquid as a dressing.

Bourbon Balls

2 teaspoons cocoa
1 cup sugar
1/4 cup bourbon
2 teaspoons white corn syrup
2 cups crushed vanilla wafers
1 cup pecans, finely chopped

Sift cocoa and sugar into a bowl. Stir in bourbon and syrup. Add the crumbs and mix well. Roll into one-inch balls. Roll in powdered sugar. Allow to dry before serving.

26

Sausage Balls with Rice Salad

Deviled Ham Dip with Sesame Crackers

Strawberry Dip with Fresh Whole Strawberries

low country
Tea Time For Ten

served with **Regular Iced or Hot Tea**

Sausage Balls With Rice Salad

1 pound mild pork sausage	1/4 cup chili sauce
1 egg, slightly beaten	1 tablespoon soy sauce
1/3 cup seasoned bread crumbs	2 tablespoons brown sugar
1/4 teaspoon sage	1 tablespoon vinegar
1/4 cup ketchup	1/2 cup water

Combine first four ingredients and shape into balls. Brown in frying pan over medium heat until all sides are brown. Remove from pan and drain on paper towels. Pour out drippings leaving about one tablespoon in pan. To drippings, stir in rest of ingredients. Return sausage balls to pan when sauce is thoroughly heated. Cover and simmer for thirty minutes.

Deviled Ham Dip with Sesame Crackers

2-21/4 cans deviled ham
1/2 cup sour cream
1 cup mayonnaise
1/2 teaspoon paprika
3 tablespoons chopped green onions
11/4 teaspoons Worcestershire sauce

Combine all ingredients; mix well. Place in bowl on serving tray along with sesame crackers. Sprinkle additional paprika on dip, if desired.

Strawberry Dip with Fresh Whole Strawberries

1 (8 ounce) package cream cheese
1 (6 ounce) jar marshmallow creme
1/2 teaspoon butternut-vanilla flavoring
Fresh whole strawberries with stems

Cream the cheese and marshmallow creme together until light and fluffy. Add flavoring, beating for a few more seconds.
Place in a decorative bowl on platter and surround with the fresh strawberries.

**Rolled Anchovy
Sandwiches**

Salad Normande

Coffee Mousse

Tea For Twelve

*served
with* **Lemon Tea**

Rolled Anchovy Sandwiches

Thin sliced white bread
1 (8 ounce) package cream cheese
2 teaspoons anchovy paste
3 tablespoons sour cream
Dash of garlic powder

Trim crust from bread and flatten with rolling pin. Set aside.
Combine rest of ingredients and mix well. Spread mixture on bread
slices. Roll up jelly roll style and cut crosswise. Broil 4" away from heat
for 2-3 minutes or until nicely browned.

Salad Normande

2 quarts salad greens
1/3 cup olive oil
3 tablespoons wine vinegar
Salt to taste
1 teaspoon chopped almonds

Rinse and drain salad greens, set aside. In a shaker combine rest of
ingredients; shake well. Pour over greens just before serving.

Coffee Mousse

1 pint whipping cream
1/2 cup sugar
1/2 teaspoon vanilla
2 egg whites, stiffly beaten
2 teaspoons instant coffee

Partially whip the cream. Add the sugar, coffee and vanilla until
peaks form. Fold in beaten egg whites. Pour into oblong pan and freeze
until ready to serve. Pretty served with a dollop of whipped cream
topped with chocolate curls.

White Bread Sandwiches with
Seafood-Cucumber Filling
Brown Bread Sandwiches
with Olive Filling
Horn of Plenty Filled
with Chicken Salad
Toasted Almond Balls
Divinity Candy
Fruit Cups
Coconut Crunch Torte
Roasted Pecans
Orange & Cream Cheese
Nut Spread
Buttermilk Lemon Cake

menu
*Tea For Forty
To Fifty*

served
with Sparkling
Tea Punch

White Bread Sandwiches with Seafood-Cucumber Filling

2 cup crabmeat or shrimp
2/3 cup grated cucumber, drained (press out moisture on paper towels)
4 teaspoons minced chives
2-4 teaspoons lemon juice (fresh)
1/2 teaspoon salt
1/4 teaspoon dried dill weed
8 tablespoons Hellman's mayonnaise or regular sour cream

Combine all ingredients and chill thoroughly. Makes about 3 cups. Spread on white bread. Trimmed about 60 finger sandwiches. Do not make more than two hours ahead of time to prevent sogginess.

Brown Bread Sandwiches with Olive Filling

1/2 cup almonds or pecans
1 (4 1/2 ounces) chopped olives
1/2 teaspoon Worcestershire sauce
Salt to taste
1/2 teaspoon lemon juice
2 cups of Hellman's mayonnaise
1 loaf whole wheat bread

Chop almonds fine; combine other ingredients. Trim crust from bread. Spread sandwich filling on bread slices. Cut into 4 small finger sandwiches. Yield: about 30 finger sandwiches.

Horn of Plenty Filled with Chicken Salad

Cut white paper (purchased from store in wrapping section) in 2 1/2 inch squares. Prepare pastry dough or get already made squares at grocery store. Roll out until about 1/8 inch thick and cut into 2 1/2 inch squares. Start at corner and roll into cornucopia shape. Secure with toothpick. Place another piece of white paper rolled in cornucopia shape inside of shell to prevent collapsing. Bake on ungreased baking sheet at 425 degrees for about 10 minutes or until slightly brown. When cool slip paper out. Fill with chicken salad a short while before serving. Makes a serving for 72 or enough for a party of 50.

Chicken Salad

4 cups chopped cooked chicken
1 large can of pineapple bits, drained
2 cups seedless green grapes
2/3 cup almonds
Salt to taste

1 cup Hellman's mayonnaise
2 tablespoons lemon juice (fresh)
2 tablespoons pineapple juice
1/2 cup chopped celery

Combine chicken, pineapple, grapes, almonds and celery. Stir in salt. In another bowl, combine mayonnaise, lemon juice and pineapple juice. Fold in with chicken mixture. Will fill two horns of plenty.

Toasted Almond Balls

1 (6 ounce) package semisweet chocolate bits
1 (6 ounce) package of butterscotch bits
1/2 cup of sifted powered sugar
1/2 teaspoon almond extract
1/2 cup sour cream

1 1/2 teaspoons grated orange rind
1/4 teaspoon salt
2 cups dry cake crumbs or plain crushed cookies
1 cup almonds, toasted

Melt chocolate and butterscotch bits together over boiling water. Remove from heat. Blend in powered sugar, almond extract, sour cream, orange rind and salt. Stir in cake or cookie crumbs and chill until firm. Shape into one inch balls. Roll into chopped almonds. Put on wax paper for 30 minutes. Store in tight covered container.

Divinity Candy

3 1/2 cups sugar
1 cup corn syrup
1/2 teaspoon vanilla
4 cups water
3 egg whites. beaten stiff

Boil sugar, syrup and water until it hardens when dropped into cold water. Pour syrup real slow into beaten egg whites. Continue to beat constantly until creamy. Drop on wax paper until hard.

Fruit Cups

Cut up apples, oranges, grapes, watermelon, cantaloupe and strawberries into large bowl. Add water to cover, 1/2 cup sugar and 3 cubes of ice. Let set 1 hour in refrigerator. Drain and pour into individual cups making sure each fruit is there.

Coconut Crunch Torte

1 cup graham cracker crumbs
1/2 cup moist shredded coconut
1/2 cup chopped nuts
4 egg whites
1/4 teaspoon salt
1 teaspoon vanilla
1 teaspoon sugar
1 pint butter brickle ice cream

Combine crumbs, coconut and nuts. Beat egg whites with salt and vanilla until foamy. Gradually add sugar and continue to beat until it forms a stiff peak. Fold crumbs into egg whites. Spread in well greased pie plate. Bake at 350 degrees about 30 minutes. Remove from oven and cool. Cut into wedges and top with ice cream. Makes servings for 6. Mix according to guest list.

Roasted Pecans

Shell pecans, about 4 cups. Add 1/2 stick of butter melted and drop in nuts. Add 1/2 teaspoon of salt. Bake on cookie sheet covered with tin for about 15 minutes or until crunchy.

Orange Cream Cheese and Nut Spread

12 ounces soft cream cheese
1 1/2 cup pecans
1 cup orange marmalade

Combine cheese and orange marmalade in blender. Cover, blend until mixed. Add pecans and push down into mixture. Cover and blend only until nuts are coarsely chopped. Makes about 3 1/2 cups.

Buttermilk Lemon Cake

2 cups shortening
1 cup butter or margarine
5 cups sugar
8 eggs
7 cups flour
1 teaspoon salt
2 cups buttermilk
2 teaspoons lemon extract
1 teaspoon soda
2 tablespoons hot water

Topping:
1 cup sugar
1 cup hot water
Juice and rind of 2 lemons

Cream shortening, butter and sugar until fluffy. Add eggs one at a time and beat. Alternate flour sifted with salt and buttermilk mixed with extract. Add soda dissolved in hot water. Bake 325 degrees for about 1 hour and 15 minutes in 2 tube cake pans lined in bottom with waxed paper. Cook topping until sugar is dissolved and the syrup is light. Pour over hot cake.

Tea Time

Tea time is a special time
for maybe two or ten,
It gives us time to catch up on
news and find out how we've been.

The time to say I love you,
and hope you feel the same.
To say I'm glad to have you
and so very pleased you came.
As the tea is brewing and
the flavors are all around,
We sit out in our easy chairs
and lay our worries down.

1999 Rose A. Newman

Bacon Green Salad

Cheddar Pine Spread

Cheese Dreams

Smoky Mountain Hot Bread

Lemon Apricot Cake

January 1st

new year's

Tea For Six

served with **Russian Tea**

Bacon Green Salad

1 large head lettuce
1/4 cup plus 2 tablespoons vegetable oil
3 tablespoons wine vinegar
1 1/2 teaspoons prepared mustard
1/2 pound bacon, cooked well
Crushed Italian pepper

Tear lettuce into chunks in salad bowl. Mix remaining ingredients for dressing. Just before serving, toss lettuce with dressing. Yield: 6 servings.

Cheddar Pine Spread

1 cup creamed cottage cheese
1/2 cup crushed pineapple (drained, reserve juice)
1/2 cup grated Cheddar cheese
1 tablespoon mayonnaise

Cream cottage cheese thoroughly using electric blender or mixer. (May need to add reserved juice for proper spreading consistency.) Add remaining ingredients and blend well. Use as spread for open face sandwiches.

Cheese Dreams

2 cups grated cheese
1 cup butter or margarine
3 cups flour

3/4 teaspoon salt
3/4 teaspoon paprika

Cut cheese and margarine into flour. Add seasoning. Shape into ball; place in bowl and chill. Roll thin and cut with small cutter, working with small amount of dough each time. Place pecan half on top of each biscuit. Bake at 400 degrees for 8 to 10 minutes until lightly browned. Yield: about 4 dozen.

Smoky Mountain Hot Bread

2 cups cornmeal
1/4 teaspoon soda
2 teaspoons baking powder
1 teaspoon salt
2 eggs, beaten
2 cups sour milk or buttermilk
2 tablespoons melted shortening or vegetable oil

Combine dry ingredients; add eggs, milk, and shortening. Mix well. Pour into a greased 8 inch square pan; bake at 425 degrees for 20 to 30 minutes. Serve hot. Yield: 9 servings. Note: eliminate soda, baking powder and salt if self-rising cornmeal is used.

Lemon Apricot Cake

1 box lemon cake mix
1 cup apricot nectar
3/4 cup oil

1/2 cup sugar
4 eggs

Blend together cake mix, nectar, oil and sugar. Add eggs, one at a time. Beat slightly. Bake in greased tube pan one hour at 325 degrees. Cool in pan 10 minutes.
Lemon Glaze:
Combine one cup confectioners' sugar and the juice of one lemon and pour over cake while warm. Use food coloring to tint glaze, if desired.

"My favorite time of
the year is when it's
cold outside and time
for Russian Tea."

R. Newman

Vegetable Dip with Sesame Crackers

Olive Puffs

Red & Green Pinwheels

Beef Fondue

Fondue Sauces
(gentlemen's choice,
brown mushroom & easy cheese)

February 14th
valentine's day
Tea For Lovers

served with **Hot Spiced Tea**

Vegetable Dip with Sesame Crackers

6 ounce package chive cream cheese
1/4 cup milk
1/4 teaspoon salt
1 teaspoon prepared mustard
1/2 cup chopped toasted almonds

Soften cheese with milk. Mix in rest of ingredients. Serve with cauliflowerets, carrot sticks, celery sticks and sesame crackers.

Olive Puffs

1/2 cup margarine or butter
2 cups grated cheese-sharp
1 1/4 cups flour
1 teaspoon paprika
Stuffed olives - about 48

Chill dough 15 to 20 minutes (or longer), might have to put flour on hands. Mold 1/2 teaspoon dough around dry olive. Chill overnight. Bake at 400 degrees for 10 to 12 minutes. Yield: 4 dozen.

Red and Green Pinwheels

1/2 of 3 ounce package cream cheese, softened
3 thin slices boiled ham (6x4 inches)
3 medium-sized stalks asparagus (cooked and chilled)

Cut cream cheese into 3 slices and spread one piece on each slice of ham. Trim asparagus stalks to a length of 4 inches and place stalk on each ham slice. Roll ham tightly around asparagus. Chill well. Slice each roll into 1/2 inch pieces. Place on toothpicks or, if desired, serve on crackers.

Beef Fondue

2 pounds beef tenderloin, cut in one-inch cubes
3 cups oil
1 teaspoon salt

About fifteen minutes before dinner blot cubes dry and mound on bed of greens. In electric fondue pot heat oil and salt on high. Spear cube with fondue fork; cook in hot oil. Dip cooked meat in sauce of your choice.

Fondue Sauces

Gentleman's Choice

1/2 cup mayonnaise	1 teaspoon chopped onion
1 teaspoon lemon juice	1 tablespoon horseradish

Combine all ingredients. Yield: 1/2 cup.

Brown Mushroom Sauce

2 tablespoons butter	1 tablespoon Worcestershire
2 tablespoons flour	sauce
2/3 cup beef consomme	1/2 cup chopped mushrooms
	1/2 cup sour cream

Melt butter in saucepan. Blend in flour. Gradually stir in consomme. Cook until thickens. Blend in remaining ingredients. Serve hot. Yield: 1 1/3 cups.

Easy Cheese Fondue

2 packages white sauce mix	1 cup Swiss cheese, shredded
1 cup sharp Cheddar cheese, shredded	1 1/2 teaspoons minced onion

Prepare sauce mix as directed. Turn control to medium; add cheeses, stirring constantly until melted. Add onion.

Dippers: French bread cubes, cooked shrimp, ham cubes, green peppers and cherry tomatoes.

"What better joy is there than sharing a pot of tea with the one you love."

Avocado Dip

Cream Cheese & Ginger
Sandwiches on Nut Bread

Cauliflower in a Pot

Pecan Orange Crisps

March 17th
st. patrick's day

Tea For Ten

served
with **Mint Green Tea**

Avocado Dip

2 ripe avocados, medium size
1 cup sour cream
1/4 teaspoon salt
2 tablespoons horseradish
1/4 cup grated onion

Mash avocado until smooth. Add the other ingredients and mix well. Chill 2 to 3 hours before serving. Yield: two cups.

Cream Cheese and Ginger Sandwiches on Nut Bread

(Sweet Spread-Ideal for use on banana nutbread or other sweet bread)
2 packages cream cheese
4 tablespoons chopped crystalized ginger
4 drops green food coloring
Fruit juice to moisten
Nutbread

Make a smooth paste of cream cheese, ginger, and fruit juice. Spread between thin slices of nutbread for a sweet party sandwich.

Cauliflower in a Pot

1 cauliflower head	2 cucumbers
1/2 pound cooked bacon (crisp)	2 sliced tomatoes
1/4 cup pimientos	1 can artichokes
2 teaspoons parsley	2 avocados
1/2 head lettuce	

Cook a whole cauliflower in pot. Drain thoroughly and cool; sprinkle with cooked bacon (crisp) and broken up. Combine pimiento with french dressing (chill); arrange cauliflower in center of large round platter. Surround with lettuce leaves. Fill lettuce leaves with cucumbers, sliced tomatoes, artichokes and avocados. Offer French or Thousand Island dressing. Sprinkle over with parsley. Serve with crackers or melba toast.

French Dressing Recipe:
1/2 cup sugar
1/2 cup salad oil
1/2 cup vinegar
1/2 teaspoon onion salt

Whip together until sugar dissolves; add one can tomato soup; beat well.

Pecan Orange Crisps

1 cup shortening	2 tablespoons orange juice
1/2 cup brown sugar	3 cups sifted flour
1/2 cup sugar	1/4 teaspoon salt
1 egg, beaten	1/2 teaspoon soda
2 tablespoons orange rind	1 teaspoon ginger
1/2 cup chopped pecans	

Cream together shortening and sugars. Add egg, orange rind and orange juice. Add dry ingredients, sifted together; add pecans. Mix until blended. Shape dough into rolls, 2 inches in diameter. Wrap each roll in waxed paper. Chill until firm. Cut in 1/8 inch slices. Bake on ungreased cookie sheet at 400 degrees about 7 minutes. Yield: 12 dozen.

"Kind words spoken are words you won't have to eat."

Stuffed Lettuce

Egg Dip

*Chicken Cucumber
Salad Sandwiches*

Sour Cream Crunchies

easter
Tea For Six

served
with **Regular Iced Tea**

Stuffed Lettuce

1 large head lettuce
1 cup grated Cheddar cheese
1/4 cup mayonnaise or
    salad dressing
1/4 teaspoon curry powder
1/3 cup finely cut celery

1/4 cup slivered cooked ham
    slices
1 pimiento, diced
1/4 cup snipped parsley
French dressing
    (recipe on page 71)

Wash and drain lettuce. With sharp knife, at core end of head, cut about a three inch circle. Then, continue cutting straight down to within 1/2 inch of the top of the head. Now, with fingers and knife hollow out this circle as evenly as possible, reserving pieces for later use.

In bowl, combine cheese with mayonnaise and curry until smooth. Stir in ham, celery, pimiento and parsley. Stuff mixture into hollowed-out lettuce, packing filling firmly; refrigerate until served.

To serve cut crosswise into slices - 1 inch thick. Place on salad plates. Makes 4 servings.

Variations for Filling:

Vegetable - soften 1 8-ounce package cream cheese with 1 tablespoon milk; add dash of Tabasco, 1 1/2 teaspoons horseradish, 1/4 diced pimiento, 1/4 cup snipped parsley and 1 cup canned peas.

Crunchy - soften 1 8-ounce package cream cheese with 1/4 cup mayonnaise. Stir in 1/2 cup grated carrots, 1/2 cup grated radishes, and 1/4 cup snipped chives.

Fruit - soften 1 8-ounce package cream cheese with 1 tablespoon lemon juice. Add 2 pineapple slices cut in pieces, 1/2 cup broken walnuts.

Egg Dip

2 tablespoons vinegar
2 tablespoons mustard relish
2 tablespoons mayonnaise
1/4 cup sour cream
1/4 teaspoon celery seeds

3 strips green pepper
Dash of Tabasco
Salt and pepper
6 hard cooked eggs,
    peeled, cut in quarters

Combine all ingredients, except eggs in blender. Cover, blend on low until smooth. Add eggs, cover and blend on low until eggs are chopped fine, stopping to scrape down. Chill. Makes about 1 3/4 cups.
    Note: A 2 1/4 ounce can deviled ham or 3 slices sharp cheese broken in chunks may be added with eggs before blending.

Chicken Cucumber Salad Sandwiches

2 cups ground cooked chicken
1/2 cup each minced celery and cucumber
2 tablespoons chopped capers
1/2 cup mayonnaise

Mix together well. Spread on your choice of bread.

Sour Cream Crunchies

3 1/2 cups sifted flour
1/2 teaspoon baking soda
1/2 cup soft butter or margarine
1 cup sugar

1/2 cup sour cream
1 egg
1 teaspoon vanilla
4 cups sugar frosted flakes

Sift together flour and soda. Blend butter and sugar; add sour cream, egg and vanilla; beat well. Add sifted dry ingredients; stir until smooth. Crush sugar frosted flakes slightly. Shape dough into balls, using 1 teaspoon dough for each. Roll balls in crushed flakes. Place on greased cookie sheet. Bake at 350 degrees about 14 minutes. Makes about 6 dozen cookies.

*"Life's greatest
pleasures come
from the presence
of others."*

R. Newman

Chicken Salad with Carrots

Sesame Cheese Rolls

Chocolate Cheese Cake

May
mother's day
Tea For Eight

served with **Regular Iced Tea**
after lunch **Hot Tea**

Chicken Salad with Carrots

1 tablespoon freshly squeezed lemon juice
1 cup Hellman's mayonnaise
2 cups diced cooked chicken
1 cup shredded carrots
3/4 cup diced celery
1/2 cup slivered blanched almonds
2 tablespoons finely chopped onions
Salt to taste
Lettuce

Stir lemon juice into mayonnaise. Toss with chicken, carrot, celery, almonds, onion and salt. Chill and serve on lettuce. Yield: 4 servings.

Sesame Cheese Rolls

16 slices white bread, crusts removed
1 (6 ounce) jar processed yellow cheese spread
3 tablespoons sesame seed, toasted

Use a rolling pin to flatten slices of bread. Spread each with cheese, sprinkle with sesame seed. Roll each slice, jellyroll fashion; brush with melted butter; cover with waxed paper or plastic wrap; chill several hours.
Cut rolls in half crosswise and place on baking sheet, seam-side down; bake at 425 degrees about 10 minutes, or until lightly browned. Yield: 32 small sandwiches.

Chocolate Cheesecake

(may be prepared ahead of time)

1 box thin chocolate
wafer cookies, crushed
1/4 cup butter, melted
1/4 teaspoon ground cinnamon
1 (12 ounce) package
semisweet chocolate bits

2 pounds cream cheese,
softened
2 cups sugar
4 eggs
3 teaspoons cocoa
2 teaspoons vanilla extract
2 cups commercial sour cream

Combine crushed wafers with butter and cinnamon; press into bottom and sides of a 10 inch springfoam; chill.

Melt semisweet chocolate in top of double boiler over warm water. Beat softened cheese in large mixer bowl until fluffy and smooth. Gradually beat in sugar, then eggs one at a time, beating after each addition. Add melted chocolate, cocoa, and flavoring; blend thoroughly. Stir in sour cream and pour into chilled crust. Bake at 350 degrees for 1 hour and 10 minutes. (The cake will be slightly runny but will become firm as it chills.) Cool at room temperature, then chill at least 5 hours before serving. Freezes well. Yield: 12 servings.

"To leave a good
taste in someone's
mouth is better than
any pie or cake we
could bake."

R. Newman

Herbed Cheese Dip

Baked Tomatoes

Garlic Bread

Almond Squares

June
father's day

Tea For Six

served
with **Johnny**
Appleseed **Tea**

Herbed Cheese Dip

1/4 pound Jack or white Cheddar cheese, softened
1 (8 ounce) package cream cheese, softened
1/4 cup grated Parmesan cheese
1 1/2 tablespoons soft butter
1/2 teaspoon dried marjoram, crushed
1/4 teaspoon dried tarragon, crushed
1 teaspoon grated lemon rind
Juice of 1/2 lemon
1/3 cup Chablis (or other dry white wine)

Blend cheeses with butter in large bowl of electric mixer until creamy and smooth. (You may have to add a little of the wine to loosen the mixture so it will beat more easily.) Mix marjoram, tarragon, and lemon rind in small bowl; add to cheese mixture, then gradually beat in lemon juice and wine. Turn into bowl or small, lightly oiled mold and chill thoroughly. Serve with unsalted crackers and fresh fruit.

Baked Tomatoes

Cut three large tomatoes in half crosswise; brush with melted butter; sprinkle with salt, pepper and curry powder or crushed dried basil. Wrap in aluminum foil and bake at 425 degrees about 10 minutes, or until tender. Yield: 6 servings.

Garlic Bread

1/2 cup butter or margarine, softened
1 clove garlic, minced
1 teaspoon dried parsley flakes
1/4 teaspoon oregano
1/4 teaspoon dried dill, crushed
1 loaf French bread

Combine butter, garlic, parsley flakes, oregano and dill. (Flavor is better if mixture is prepared several days before using.) Put in covered container and refrigerate. Remove for 1 hour to soften before spreading on bread. Cut bread into 3/4 inch slices, but not quite through the bottom crust. Spread butter mixture generously between slices. Wrap loosely in aluminum foil and bake at 425 degrees. Yield: 6 servings.

Almond Squares

1 cup butter (no substitute)
3/4 cup sugar
1 egg, separated
1/2 cup almond paste
1 teaspoon almond extract
2 cups all-purpose flour, sifted
1/2 cup sliced almonds

Cream butter and sugar thoroughly in large bowl of electric mixer. Add egg yolk, the almond paste, and extract. Beat well; add flour and beat just until blended; do not overbeat. Smooth with a spatula into an ungreased 12"x8"x2" inch pan or ovenproof baking dish. Beat egg white until foamy and brush over surface of dough. Scatter almonds over top and bake at 350 degrees (325 degrees for glass) for 40 minutes, until cake tests done. Cool and cut into squares. Yield: 2 to 2 1/2 dozen squares.

"Ode to the young
that's full of vigor.
Instead of growing
older and bigger
and bigger!"

R. Newman

Yankee Doodle Salad

Shrimp & Shells

Crescents

Chocolate Frosted
Shortbread

fourth of july
Tea For Eight

*served
with* Mint Iced Tea

Yankee Doodle Salad

3/4 cup vinegar
3/4 cup sugar
4 tablespoons water
1/2 cup cooking oil
1/4 cup chopped onions

1/2 cup chopped celery
1 teaspoon salt
3 teaspoons paprika
Dash pepper
1 large can french green beans
2 cups canned green peas

Mix all ingredients except peas and beans. Then add peas and beans to the marinade. Refrigerate 24 hours. Drain and serve on lettuce cups. Serves 8.

Shrimp and Shells

3 pounds uncooked shrimp in the shell
4 tablespoons butter or margarine
2 (4 ounce) can sliced mushrooms, drained; or
    1 pint fresh mushrooms
2 tablespoons all-purpose flour
2 (10 ounce) cans condensed cream of shrimp soup
2 cups commercial sour cream
2 tablespoons finely minced parsley
3 tablespoons minced chives, or 4 tablespoons chopped green onion
Dash pepper
Buttered breadcrumbs

Boil, shell and clean shrimp. Heat butter in skillet and saute canned mushrooms a few minutes. (If using fresh mushrooms, saute as follows: chop stems, put in skillet with hot butter, and saute for about 3 minutes; then add sliced mushroom caps and saute about 2 minutes.) Stir in flour, blend in soup, stirring constantly until smooth and thick. Blend in sour cream, parsley and chives and when smooth again; add shrimp. Add pepper and taste to check seasonings. Turn into four large shells or ramekins, sprinkle with buttered crumbs and bake at 375 degrees for 15 to 20 minutes. Do not overbake. Yield: 4 generous servings.

Crescents

1 cake compressed yeast or 1 package dry yeast
1 teaspoon sugar
3/4 cup milk, scalded
2 eggs, beaten
3/4 cup butter or margarine
1/3 cup sugar
3/4 teaspoon salt
4 cups all-purpose flour

In a small bowl dissolve yeast and 1 teaspoon sugar in 1/4 cup of milk which has been cooled to lukewarm (very warm for dry yeast). Add eggs; mix well. Cream butter with 1/3 cup sugar and salt in large bowl of electric mixer; combine with first mixture. Add half the flour, then remaining milk, then rest of flour. Beat until dough is smooth. Turn into greased bowl, grease top of dough lightly, cover with light cloth and place in warm spot to rise until double in bulk. Punch dough down, cover and chill for an hour or two for easier handling.

Divide dough in half. Roll out each portion into a 16 inch circle about 1/4 inch thick. Cut into quarters; then cut each quarter into four parts, yielding 16 triangular pieces from each half of dough.

Beginning at wide edge of triangle, roll tightly toward the point, shape into crescents and place, pointed end down, on greased baking sheet. Cover with light cloth and let rise until not quite double in bulk. Bake at 375 degrees for about 15 minutes, or until light golden. Serve warm. Yield: 32 rolls.

Chocolate Frosted Shortbread

2 cups flour
1/2 cup brown sugar
1 (6 ounce) package semisweet chocolate pieces
3/4 cup butter or margarine
2/3 cup nuts, chopped fine

Mix flour and sugar; cut in butter until mixture resembles coarse cornmeal. Press firmly into ungreased 15"x10"x1" pan. Bake 25 to 28 minutes at 325 degrees. Melt chocolate; spread over hot, baked layer. Sprinkle nuts over chocolate and press gently. Cut into squares while warm. Yield: 70 cookies.

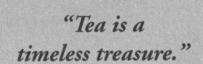

*"Tea is a
timeless treasure."*

S. Strickland

**Asparagus &
Lettuce Salad with
French Dressing**

Breadsticks

**Low Calorie
Baked Alaska**

August rose &
sharon's birthday

*Tea Time Diet
Style For
Four-Six*

*served
with* **Peach Tea**

Asparagus and Lettuce Salad with French Dressing

1 head of lettuce
1 cup asparagus tips, canned and drained
1 cup pickled or plain beets, canned and drained
1 cup summer peas, frozen and cooked for 3 minutes
1 cup cauliflower, cooked and cooled
2 sliced tomatoes

Place 5 lettuce leaves around plate with cup in center. Fill with above vegetables.

Center Cup:

2 cups boiled and chopped ham
1 cup diced celery
2 hard boiled eggs, chopped
2 tablespoons chopped pimiento
1/2 teaspoon paprika
1/2 teaspoon of salt

Combine and add mayonnaise to right consistency; add french dressing (see recipe below). Serve with crackers or hot rolls.

French Dressing

1 can tomato soup
1/2 cup sugar
2 tablespoons Worcestershire sauce
2 tablespoons mustard
1/2 teaspoon salt
1/2 teaspoon pepper
1/2 cup vinegar
1/2 teaspoon garlic salt
1 cup cooking oil

Place all ingredients except oil in blender. Blend well; add oil and blend until mixed. Yield: 2 1/2 cups.

Breadsticks

Remove crust from bread and cut each slice into 4 strips. Spread softened butter or margarine on each breadstick. Put on a baking sheet; toast at 450 degrees or until lightly browned.

Low Calorie Baked Alaska

1 quart flavored yogurt, softened
1 baked 9 inch pastry shell
Meringue (recipe follows)

Spoon ice cream into pastry shell; spread to edge and level top. Freeze until serving time. Preheat over to 425 degrees. When ready to serve, cover completely with meringue. Bake 3 to 4 minutes or until meringue is lightly browned. Serve immediately. Yield: 6 to 8 servings.

Meringue:

3 egg whites
1/4 teaspoon cream of tartar
6 tablespoons sugar

Beat egg whites until foamy. Add cream of tartar and beat until soft peaks form. Add sugar, 1 tablespoon at a time. Continue beating until shiny peaks form. Yield: meringue for one 9 inch pie.

*"Loving memories
of others is like
eating our favorite
candy bar."*

R. Newman

Chilled Fruit in Wine

Labor Day Salad

Cheese Garlic Bread

Apple Brown Betty

September

labor day

Tea For Six

served with **Cranberry Tea**

Chilled Fruit in Wine

1/2 cup sugar
1/2 cup water
1/2 Burgundy or Bordeaux wine
1 pint strawberries
1 pint blueberries
1 pint red raspberries

Combine sugar, water and wine in saucepan; bring to a boil. Lower heat and simmer 5 minutes. Put strawberries, blueberries and raspberries in a glass bowl; pour wine syrup over fruit and chill until ready to serve. Yield: 6 to 8 servings.

Labor Day Salad

1 head lettuce, torn into bite-size pieces
1/4 cup Swiss cheese strips
1/4 cup sliced radishes
1 or 2 tomatoes, cut into wedges
Chopped parsley
1 teaspoon dry mustard
1 teaspoon seasoned salt
1/2 teaspoon paprika
1/4 teaspoon garlic juice
1/4 cup wine vinegar
1/2 cup olive oil

Toss lettuce, cheese, radishes, tomatoes and parsley in salad bowl. Chill. Combine mustard, salt, paprika and garlic juice in a mixing bowl and mix well; add vinegar. Add olive oil very slowly, beating constantly until all oil is added. Add dressing to vegetables just before serving. Yield: 6 servings.

Cheese Garlic Bread

1/2 cup butter or margarine, softened
1/2 teaspoon garlic salt
1/3 cup grated Parmesan cheese
1 teaspoon Worcestershire sauce
1/4 teaspoon cayenne pepper
1 (1 pound) loaf French bread

Whip butter; blend in garlic salt, cheese, Worcestershire sauce and cayenne pepper. Slice French bread into 1/4 inch slices. Butter both sides of each slice. Broil 1 minute on each side of toast in oven. Yield: 6 to 8 servings.
Note: Bread may be wrapped in foil and heated on the grill.

Apple Brown Betty

1 (28 ounce) can applesauce
2 bananas, sliced
1 cup firmly packed light brown sugar
1/3 cup melted butter or margarine
1/2 cup graham cracker crumbs
Cream or vanilla ice cream

Combine first 5 ingredients; pour into a greased 1 1/2 quart shallow baking dish. Bake at 325 degrees for 35 minutes. Serve warm with cream or vanilla ice cream. Yield: 6 servings.

"We met over a
cup of tea and a
special friend you
turned out to be."

Sharon Strickland

Sin Salad

Hot Beer Bread

Ice Box Fruit Cake

October
october festival
For Six-Eight

served
with **Hot Spiced Tea**

Sin Salad

1 package lime gelatin	1 #2 can crushed pineapple,
2 cups boiling water	drained
2 cups miniature marshmallows	3/4 cup nuts, chopped
1 cup sharp Cheddar cheese,	2 tablespoons lemon juice
grated	1/2 pint cream, whipped
1 1/2 cups celery, chopped	1/3 cup mayonnaise

Stir gelatin and marshmallows into hot water until melted. Chill until mixture begins to thicken. Add cheese, celery, pineapple, nuts and lemon juice. Combine whipped cream and mayonnaise and add to mixture. Pour into an 8"x12"x2" dish. Refrigerate for at least 12 hours. Yield: 6-8 servings.

Hot Beer Bread

3 cups self-rising flour
3 tablespoons sugar
1 (12 ounce) can beer, at room temperature
2 teaspoons melted butter

Mix all ingredients. Pour batter into buttered loadpan. Bake at 350 degrees for 50 minutes. Brush top with melted butter, if desired. Yield: 1 loaf.

Ice Box Fruit Cake

1 package graham crackers	1 box light raisins
1 bag small marshmallows	1 large jar cherries
1 large can evaporated milk	1 1/2 pound shelled pecans
1 package frozen coconut	

Crush crackers in a large bowl. Set aside. Combine canned milk and half of a bag of marshmallows. In a heavy saucepan, cook on low stirring constantly until marshmallows have dissolved. Pour over cracker crumbs. Add rest of marshmallows and other ingredients; mix well. Pour into airtight oblong container and press flat. Refrigerate 2-3 days before serving. Double recipe for large crowd.

Cheese Tarts

Crabmeat Canape

Eggplant Sticks

Orange Angel Cake

November

thanksgiving

served with **Hot Orange Tea**

Cheese Tarts

2 cups (8 ounces) shredded sharp Cheddar cheese
1 tablespoon half-and-half
1/2 teaspoon dry mustard
1/4 teaspoon paprika
1/2 teaspoon Worcestershire sauce
1/4 teaspoon hot sauce (optional)
24 (1 inch) baked commercial tart shells

Combine cheese, half-and-half, mustard, paprika, Worcestershire sauce and hot sauce in top of double boiler; heat over hot water, stirring occasionally, until cheese melts. Spoon into tart shells; allow to stand 10 minutes before serving. Yield: 24 appetizers.

Crabmeat Canapes

1/2 cup mayonnaise
1/2 teaspoon prepared mustard
1 teaspoon Worcestershire sauce
2 teaspoons grated horseradish
1 (6 1/2 ounce) can crabmeat, drained and flaked
1/2 cup grated Parmesan cheese
Assorted party crackers or party bread

Combine mayonnaise, mustard, Worcestershire sauce, horseradish, crabmeat and Parmesan cheese; mix well. Spread on crackers. Bake at 300 degrees about 3 to 4 minutes or until heated through. Yield: about 50 appetizers.

Eggplant Sticks

1 large eggplant
All-purpose flour
Salt and pepper to taste

Peel eggplant and cut into 2 x 1/2 inch sticks. Season flour with salt and pepper. Dredge eggplant in flour. Fry in hot oil until golden brown; drain well. Serve warm. Yield: 6 servings.

Orange Angel Cake

8 large fresh oranges
2 layers of sponge cake
1 pint whipping cream
2 tablespoons sugar
4 tablespoons chopped pecans

Peel and section oranges, removing sectional fibers. Crumble sponge cake. Whip cream; add sugar. In large serving bowl place alternate layers of cake crumbles, orange sections and whipped cream. Sprinkle nuts over final topping of whipped cream.

*"A good cup of tea
is worth its
weight in gold."*

R. Newman

Christmas Salad

Ham Loaf with Sauce

Onion Bread

Mousse Filled Crepes with Hot Chocolate Sauce

December

christmas

For Twentyfive

served with **Iced Red Zinger Tea**

Christmas Salad

Eggnog Layer:

2 #2 cans crushed pineapple
2 tablespoons unflavored
   gelatin

6 tablespoons fresh lime juice
3 cups dairy eggnog
1 1/2 cups finely chopped celery

Drain pineapple syrup into saucepan; soften gelatin in syrup. Add lime juice; heat until gelatin dissolves. Cool. Add eggnog; chill until partially set. Fold in pineapple and celery. Turn into a 7 cup salad mold and chill until set.

Cranberry Layer:

2 packages raspberry flavor gelatin
3 cups boiling water
2 packages (10 ounces) cranberry-orange relish

Dissolve gelatin in boiling water. Add cranberry-orange relish. Chill until partially set. Pour over eggnog layer. Chill. Yield: 25 servings.

Ham Loaf with Sauce

4 pounds smoked,
   minced ham
2 pounds ground pork
6 eggs

2 cups fresh bread crumbs,
   softened in milk
Dry mustard to taste
Black pepper to taste

Mix all ingredients. Bake in a 375 degree oven for 1 1/2 - 1 3/4 hours or until well done.

Sauce:

2/3 cup sugar
1 cup vinegar
8 teaspoons dry mustard
1 quart cream

Salt to taste
6 egg yolks, beaten
Paprika

Blend dry ingredients; add to beaten egg yolks. Add cream; cook slowly in double boiler, stirring constantly until mixture thickens. Serve in individual small serving cups for each guest to dip in.

Onion Bread

2/3 cup very warm water
4 packages active (dry or cake) yeast
2 (10 1/2 ounce) cans condensed onion soup, undiluted
8 cups packaged biscuit mix
4 teaspoons sesame seeds
1/2 cup grated Cheddar cheese
1/2 cup melted butter or margarine

Into very warm water, in small bowl, sprinkle yeast and stir until it is dissolved. Add onion soup. Stir into biscuit mix in bowl until well blended. Pour butter or margarine into a 12"x8"x2" baking dish; sprinkle with 1 teaspoon sesame seeds, cool. Spread batter evenly over butter. Sprinkle with cheese and 1 teaspoon sesame seeds. Cover with towel and let rise in warm place about 1/2 hour or until double. May be served as hot bread or split as buns for hamburgers. Bake 400 degrees for 25 minutes or until done.

Mousse-Filled Crepes with Hot Chocolate Sauce

Dessert Crepes:

3 eggs
1/4 cup sugar
3/4 cup flour
1 1/2 cups milk or
    part cream/part milk

2 tablespoons butter, melted
    and cooled
Pinch of salt
1 tablespoon brandy or liqueur
    or 1/2 teaspoon vanilla

Beat eggs and add sugar and flour, with a little milk. Add remaining milk, cooled butter, salt and brandy. Allow to stand for at least 1 hour. Butter a 5 inch crepe pan and heat until butter bubbles. Pour in about 1 1/2 tablespoon batter, swirling it swiftly around the pan so the bottom is covered. Cook until light on 1 side (about one minute). Turn crepe over and cook on the other side for about half a minute. Stack with waxed paper in between. To freeze, put in freezer bags and seal. To defrost, set at room temperature for a short time. They can be refrozen and defrosted again without harm. Yield: 30 to 36/5 inch crepes.

(continued)

Filling:
>   1 (6 3/4 ounce) package instant chocolate or
>   chocolate fudge pudding mix
>   1 teaspoon instant coffee powder
>   2 quarts (8 cups) whipping cream, divided

Combine pudding mix and coffee powder in large bowl and blend well. Stir in 1 quart whipping cream and mix until smooth. Whip remaining cream until stiff. Gently fold into chocolate mixture, blending thoroughly. (Filling can be made 2 days ahead to this point and refrigerated. Divide among crepes and roll to enclose). Stack seam side down on serving platters (can be done 1 day ahead). Cover and chill.

Hot Chocolate Sauce

>   4 ounces bittersweet chocolate
>   1/2 cup unsalted butter
>   2 1/3 cups powdered sugar
>   1 1/4 cups evaporated milk
>   1 teaspoon vanilla
>   1 teaspoon mint or rum extract

Melt chocolate with butter in medium saucepan over low heat. Remove from heat and stir in sugar and milk, blending well. Place over medium heat and bring to boil. Reduce heat and simmer 8 minutes, stirring constantly. Remove from heat and stir in vanilla and rum. Serve warm. (Sauce can be prepared 1 week ahead and chilled.) Reheat gently, stirring often. Drizzle over crepes.

Tortes, Tarts, Mousses, Souffles, Cakes & Dainty Cookies

The following pages are truly a treat.
Desserts for any host or hostess to be proud of.

Walk through the world of tortes, tarts,
mousses, souffles, cakes and dainty cookies.
Use your imagination to make them your very
own with garnishes of your choice.

The recipes are ours, along with a few from
special friends and family. Some are quiet old
and others are updated as well as up to date.
Take time to read, imagine and create.

A true tea is a thing of dignified beauty.
Rose and Sharon

Low Calorie Banana Torte

12 graham crackers,
  crushed
2 tablespoons melted
  margarine
3/4 cup plain yogurt
1 cup drained unsweetened
  pineapple

2 bananas, chopped
1 small package low-calorie
  vanilla instant pudding mix
1/2 cup skim milk
1 1/2 cups whipped topping

Mix cracker crumbs and margarine in dish. Press evenly into dish. Mix yogurt; pineapple and bananas in bowl. Combine pudding mix and milk in bowl; mix well with fork. Add to fruit; mix well. Spoon into prepared 8"x8" dish. Top with whipped topping. Chill for several hours. One or 2 packets of Equal may be added, if desired. This easy recipe must be made several hours ahead. Yield: 9 servings.

Date Pecan Torte

1 cup boiling water
3/4 cup finely chopped dates
1 teaspoon soda
1 teaspoon butter, softened
1 cup sugar
1 egg
1 1/2 cups flour
1 teaspoon baking powder
1/2 cup chopped pecans
2 cups whipping cream
1/4 cup sugar

Pour boiling water over dates and soda in bowl. Let stand for several minutes. Beat butter, 1 cup sugar and egg in mixer bowl until light. Stir in date mixture. Add flour, baking powder and pecans; mix well. Spoon into two greased 8" cake pans. Bake at 375 degrees for 45 to 60 minutes or until cake tests done. Remove to wire rack to cool. Beat whipping cream in mixer bowl until soft peaks form. Mix in 1/4 cup sugar. Spread between layers and over top and side of cake. Store in refrigerator. This easy and special holiday cake can be frozen. Yield: 16 servings.

Blueberry Torte

1/2 cup butter, melted
2 cups sugar
36 graham crackers, rolled
2 (8 ounce) packages cream cheese
4 eggs, well beaten
1 teaspoon vanilla
Cinnamon to taste (optional)
1 1/2 to 2 cans blueberry pie mix
1 tablespoon lemon juice

Combine butter, 1 cup sugar and graham crackers; line one 9"x16" or two 9"x 9" pans with mixture. Add cream cheese to eggs; add remaining sugar and vanilla. Pour into crumb-lined pan. Bake at 375 degrees for 15 to 20 minutes or until firm. Sprinkle with cinnamon; pour pie filling mixed with lemon juice over top. Chill overnight. Top with whipped cream.

Coconut Crunch Torte

1 cup graham cracker crumbs
1/2 cup moist shredded coconut
1/2 cup chopped nuts
4 egg whites
1/4 teaspoon salt
1 teaspoon vanilla
1 cup sugar
1 pint butter brickle ice cream

Combine crumbs, coconut and nuts. Beat egg whites with salt and vanilla until foamy; gradually add sugar and continue beating until whites form still peaks. Fold crumb mixture into egg white mixture. Spread in well greased 9 inch pie plate. Bake at 350 degrees about 30 minutes. Cool. Cut in wedges; top with ice cream. Yield: 6 servings.

Soda Cracker Torte

1 cup sugar
1 cup chopped walnuts
1/8 teaspoon salt
1/2 teaspoon grated lemon rind
1/2 teaspoon almond flavoring
1/2 teaspoon cinnamon
3/4 cup broken soda crackers
3 egg whites, stiffly beaten
1/2 cup whipping cream
l/2 cup fruit cocktail, thoroughly drained

Mix sugar, walnuts, salt, lemon rind, almond flavoring, cinnamon and soda crackers. Fold in egg whites; pour into well-greased 8 inch pie pan. Spread mixture around bottom and sides of pan. Bake at 350 degrees for 25 minutes. Cool. Whip cream until stiff. Fold in fruit cocktail; spread on top of crust. Put in refrigerator until serving time. Yield: 5 servings.

Apple Torte

1 egg
3/4 cup sugar
3/4 cup pared sliced apples
1 teaspoon baking powder
1/4 teaspoon almond extract
1/2 cup flour
1/4 teaspoon salt
1/4 cup chopped nuts

Beat egg lightly; add sugar and apples. Stir in remaining ingredients. Mix well; pour into a greased 8 inch pie tin. Bake in 325 degree oven for 25 minutes. Serve with whipped cream, if desired. Yield: 4 servings.

Baked Cherry Torte

1 No. 303 can cherries	1 teaspoon cinnamon
1 cup flour	1 tablespoon melted butter
1 1/4 cup sugar	1 egg
1/4 teaspoon salt	1 teaspoon almond flavoring
1/2 teaspoon soda	1/2 cup chopped pecan meats

Drain cherries reserving juice for sauce. Mix flour, sugar, salt, soda, cinnamon, butter, cherries, egg and flavoring. Put 1/4 cup pecans into batter; mix well. Turn into a greased 9"x 9"x 2" pan. Sprinkle remaining pecans on top. Bake at 350 degrees for 45 minutes.

Sauce:

1 cup cherry juice
1 cup sugar
1 tablespoon flour
1 teaspoon almond flavoring
Red food coloring

Combine juice, sugar and flour. Cook until thick. Remove from heat; add flavoring and 3 or 4 drops red food coloring. Cool. Serve over dessert with ice cream. Yield: 9 servings.

Date Apple Torte

4 cups diced apples	1 tablespoon melted butter
1 cup sugar	1 teaspoon vanilla
1/2 cup flour	1/2 cup chopped nuts
2 teaspoons baking powder	1/2 cup chopped dates
1 egg	

Combine all ingredients in mixing bowl; stir until mixed. Do not beat. Pour into greased 8 inch square pan. Bake at 400 degrees 40 minutes. Serve hot or cold with cream, whipped cream, or ice cream. Yield: 8 servings.

Fruit Torte

1 cup sugar	1 cup sifted flour
1/4 to 1/2 teaspoon salt	1 teaspoon baking soda
1 teaspoon vanilla (optional)	1 beaten egg
2 cups fruit cocktail and juice	

Sift dry ingredients; mix well with vanilla and egg. Fold in fruit. Pour into greased 8" x 11" glass baking dish. Spread over top, 1 cup dark brown sugar mixed with 1/2 to 1 cup chopped walnuts. Bake 40 to 60 minutes at 325 degrees. Serve with whipped cream. Yield: 12-15 servings.

Rhubarb Torte

Flour	2 1/4 cups uncooked rhubarb,
Sugar	cut small
1/3 cup butter	1/4 teaspoon nutmeg
1/3 cup light cream	2 1/4 teaspoon cream of tartar
3 eggs, separated	

Mix 1 cup flour and 2 tablespoons sugar; cut in butter. Press into 9"x 9" pan. Bake at 325 degrees for 20 minutes. Combine 1 cup sugar, 2 tablespoons flour, cream, egg yolks, rhubarb and nutmeg; cook until thick. Pour over baked crust. Beat egg whites with cream of tartar until stiff. Add 6 tablespoons sugar gradually, continue beating until thick and glossy. Pile meringue on filling. Return to oven to brown meringue. Yield: 8 servings.

Frozen Pineapple Torte

3 eggs, separated	2 tablespoons lemon juice
Dash of salt	1 (9 ounce) can crushed
1/2 cup plus	pineapple, drained
2 tablespoons sugar	1 cup heavy cream, whipped
Pineapple syrup	2 cups graham cracker crumbs

Beat together egg yolks, salt and 1/2 cup sugar; add pineapple syrup and lemon juice. Cook over hot water until mixture coats spoon, stirring constantly. Add pineapple; cool. Make a meringue of stiffly beaten egg

(continued)

whites and 2 tablespoons sugar. Fold in whipped cream and custard mixture. Coat sides and bottom of greased refrigerator tray with half of cracker crumbs. Pour in custard mixture; cover with remaining crumbs. Freeze until firm, about 3 to 4 hours. Yield: 6-8 servings.

Butter Cream Torte

2 cups crushed vanilla wafers
1/2 pound butter
2 cups sifted powdered sugar
4 eggs
1/2 cup chopped almonds
1 cup whipped cream
1/4 cup chopped red maraschino cherries
1/4 cup chopped green maraschino cherries

Spread 1 cup crushed vanilla wafers in 9 inch square cake pan. Combine softened butter with sifted powdered sugar; cream well. Beat in an egg at a time. Stir in finely chopped almonds. Spoon mixture evenly over crushed wafers in cake pan. Sprinkle 3/4 cup crushed wafers on top. Beat cream until thick; fold in cherries. Spread over wafers. Sprinkle remaining crushed wafers over whipped cream. Garnish with whole cherries. Chill for 12 hours. Cut with knife dipped in water. Yield: 10-12 servings.

Chocolate Icebox Torte

2 1/2 cups graham cracker crumbs
1/2 cup sifted powdered sugar
1 teaspoon cinnamon
3/4 cup melted butter

Combine ingredients. Line bottom and sides of 10 inch torte pan with mixture. Use pan that is 2 1/2" deep. Bake at 350 degrees for 15 minutes. Cool.

(continued)

Filling:

2 envelopes unflavored gelatin
1/2 cup cold water
4 squares bitter chocolate
1 cup boiling water
8 eggs, separated

2 cups sugar
1/2 cup toasted chopped
   pecans
2 teaspoons vanilla

Dissolve gelatin in cold water. Cut chocolate into small pieces. Pour boiling water over chocolate, stirring until melted. Add gelatin mixture. Beat egg yolks well; add 1 cup sugar. Stir into chocolate mixture. Add pecans and vanilla. Beat egg whites until very stiff while slowly adding 1 cup sugar. Fold whites into chocolate mixture. Pour into crust and chill thoroughly. Yield: 20 servings.

Peach Almond Torte

1 cup vanilla wafer crumbs
2 tablespoons butter, melted
3/4 teaspoon almond extract
1 (1 pound) can sliced
   Freestone peaches
3 tablespoon unflavored gelatin
3 cups milk
1/2 cup (firmly packed)
   light brown sugar

1/8 teaspoon salt
3 egg yolks, beaten
2 teaspoons vanilla
1/2 teaspoon almond extract
3 egg whites
1/4 cup white sugar
1 cup whipping cream, whipped
1/4 cup toasted almond slices
Fresh strawberries

Place crumbs in a small bowl; stir in butter and 1/4 teaspoon almond extract. Press mixture firmly on bottom of 9 inch springform pan. Bake in a preheated 350 degree oven for 5 minutes and cool on wire rack. Drain peaches, reserving 3/4 cup syrup. Chop peaches; set aside. Sprinkle gelatin on peach syrup to soften. In a 3 quart saucepan, heat milk, brown sugar, salt and softened gelatin until gelatin is dissolved. Blend small amount of hot milk mixture into egg yolks; return to pan. Cool 2 additional minutes, stir in vanilla and remaining almond extract. Chill until partially set. Beat egg whites until frothy; gradually beat in white sugar until stiff peaks form. Fold into gelatin mixture with whipped cream. Fold in peaches and 2 tablespoons almonds. Mound into crust; sprinkle remaining almond on top. Chill. Garnish with strawberries.

Choco-Mint Torte

1 cup egg whites
1/4 teaspoon salt
1/2 teaspoon cream of tartar
2 cups sugar
1 teaspoon vanilla
2 to 3 drops peppermint extract
Chocolate Filling

Add salt and cream of tartar to egg whites, beat until soft peaks form. Add sugar gradually, beating well after each addition. Add flavorings and continue beating until sugar dissolves and mixture is stiff and shiny. Invert three 9 inch round or 8 inch square cake pans and generously grease bottoms. Lightly dust with flour. Spread meringue evenly on pans to within 1/4 inch of edge. Do not form rim. Bake at 275 degrees for 1 hour. Turn off oven and leave meringues in until oven has cooled. Remove one layer carefully to serving plate. Spread with 1/3 filling. Top with second meringue and spread with 1/3 of filling. Top with third meringue and spread with remaining filling. Chill for several hours or overnight. Just before serving, garnish with whipped cream and crushed peppermint candy. Serves 10.

Chocolate Filling:

2 squares unsweetened chocolate
2 cups coffee cream
1 cup sugar
1/4 cup flour
1/4 teaspoon salt
6 egg yolks, slightly beaten
1 1/2 teaspoons vanilla
1/2 cup heavy cream, whipped

Combine chocolate and cream in heavy saucepan and heat to scalding over medium heat. Combine sugar, flour and salt. Gradually mix hot cream into dry ingredients. Return to heat and cook until thick, stirring constantly. Remove from heat and add slowly to egg yolks, mixing well. Cook 2 to 3 minutes longer, stirring vigorously. Add vanilla; chill. Whip this mixture and fold into whipped cream.

Southern Torte Squares

1/2 pound butter (2 sticks)
1 cup sugar
6 egg yolks
2 cups flour
1 teaspoon salt
1 teaspoon baking powder
Grape jelly

Cream butter and sugar. Add the 6 egg yolks and cream well. Sift flour, salt and baking powder; add to creamed mixture. Pat this mixture on a cookie sheet and spread top surface with grape jelly. Top this with icing (recipe follows).

Icing:
6 egg whites
1 cup ground nuts
1 cup sugar

Beat egg whites until they hold peaks. Add nuts and sugar; blend well. Use this on top of torte. Cut in squares and bake for 30 minutes at 375 degrees.

Frozen Peach Torte

2 cups well mashed peaches (fresh or frozen)
1 cup sugar
1 tablespoon lemon juice
1 cup heavy cream, whipped
1 cup macaroon crumbs, coarsely crushed

Combine peaches, sugar and lemon juice. Fold in whipped cream. Place half of crumbs in a freezing tray. Pour in peach mixture. Top with remaining crumbs. Freeze until firm. Cut into squares.

Apple Torte

First Layer:

1/2 cup butter   1/2 teaspoon vanilla
1/3 tablespoon sugar   1 cup flour

Cream ingredients and spread on to bottom of 9" springfoam pan sprayed with non-stick spray.

Layer Two:

8 ounce package cream cheese   1 egg
1/3 cup sugar   1 teaspoon vanilla

Cream together and spread over first layer.

Layer Three:

3 cups thinly sliced apples
1/3 cup sugar
Cinnamon to taste

Mix all ingredients together and place on top of second layer. Sprinkle top with sliced almonds. Bake at 450 degrees for 10 minutes. Decrease to 400 degrees and bake additional 25 minutes. Cool before removing rim.

Fruit Tart

2 cups biscuit mix
1/3 cup sugar
1/3 cup margarine
1 egg
3 ounce package cream cheese
1/3 cup sugar
1 teaspoon vanilla
3/4 cup whipping cream
Fresh strawberries

Mix together first 3 ingredients. Add egg. Mix dough until soft. Pat onto a 12" pizza pan. Bake in preheated 375 degree oven for 10-12 minutes.

Beat cream cheese, sugar and vanilla. Beat in the whipping cream (already whipped). Beat until well blended. Spread on cookie crust. Arrange sliced fruit on top.

Cherry Torte with Sauce

1 cup flour	1 (No. 2) can cherries, well
1 1/2 cup soda	drained
1 teaspoon cinnamon	1 egg, beaten
1/2 teaspoon salt	1 tablespoon melted butter
1/2 cup chopped nuts	

Sift flour, sugar, soda, cinnamon and salt together. Stir in nuts. Mix cherries, egg and butter. Add to dry ingredients; mix well. Spread in greased 7"x 11" pan. Bake for 45 minutes at 350 degrees.

Sauce:

1 tablespoon cornstarch	1 cup cherry juice
1/2 teaspoon salt	1 tablespoon butter
1/2 cup sugar	Few drops of red coloring

Mix cornstarch, salt and sugar. Add cherry juice; stir till smooth. Cook over low heat until thick. Add butter and red coloring. Cut torte in squares; top with sauce and whipped cream. Yield: 8-10 servings.

Christmas Icebox Torte

1 pound powdered sugar
1/2 cup butter
4 eggs, separated
1 teaspoon vanilla
32 ladyfingers, split
1 (No. 2) can crushed pineapple, well drained
1 (10 ounce) can maraschino cherries, well drained and cut
1 pint whipping cream, whipped stiff

Cream sugar and butter until light and fluffy. Add egg yolks, 1 at a time, beating well after each addition. Fold in stiffly beaten egg whites and vanilla. Cover bottom of torte pan with ladyfingers; spread with thin layer of butter mixture. Sprinkle with half the pineapple and half the cherries. Add layer of cream. Repeat, ending with thin layer of butter mixture. Refrigerate for 24 hours. Loosen torte from side of pan. May garnish each serving with 1 tablespoon whipped cream, if desired. Yield: 16 servings.

Almond Torte

4 eggs, separated
1 cup sugar
1 teaspoon vanilla
1 cup almonds, ground fine
1 teaspoon baking powder
9 sweet zwieback rusks, ground
1 cup frozen or fresh strawberries
2 cups whipped cream, sweetened and flavored to taste

Cream egg yolks, sugar and vanilla; add almonds and baking powder to zwieback. Add to egg yolk mixture; fold in stiffly beaten egg whites. Place in 2 greased heart shaped layer tins. Bake at 350 degrees for 30 minutes. Cool; remove from tins. Spread strawberries on bottom layer; top with 1 cup cream. Add top layer; spread with remaining cream. Yield: 6 servings.

Nut Torte

4 eggs, separated
1 1/2 cups sugar
1/4 cup flour
2 teaspoons baking powder
1/2 teaspoon salt
1 teaspoon vanilla
3 cups chopped nuts
1/2 gallon vanilla ice cream
Crushed strawberries

Beat egg whites until stiff; beat in 3/4 cup sugar. Beat egg yolks; add remaining sugar, flour, baking powder and salt. Fold into egg white mixture; fold in vanilla and nuts. Pour into greased and floured baking sheet. Bake at 350 degrees for 35 to 40 minutes. Cool; top with ice cream. Place in freezer until served. Cut into squares; top with strawberries just before serving. Yield: 12 servings.

Strawberry Torte

1 cup sifted cake flour
1 teaspoon baking powder
1/4 teaspoon salt
2 eggs
1 cup sugar
1 teaspoon vanilla

1/2 cup milk
1 tablespoon butter
1 pint fresh strawberries
2 cups frozen whipped topping,
   thawed

Sift flour with baking powder and salt. Beat eggs in small bowl until thick and light in color, about 5 minutes. Add sugar, 1 tablespoon at a time, beating thoroughly after each addition; add vanilla. Add flour mixture, a small amount at a time, blending by hand or at low speed of electric mixer. Bring milk and butter to a boil; stir quickly into flour mixture, blending thoroughly. Pour quickly into 8 inch square pan which has been greased and floured on bottom only. Bake at 350 degrees for 25 to 30 minutes or until cake tester inserted into center comes out clean. Cool cake in pan for 10 minutes; remove from pan. Finish cooling on rack. Cut half the strawberries in halves. Split cooled cake in half horizontally, making 2 layers. Spread 1/2 cup whipped topping on one layer; top with halved strawberries. Top with remaining layer; spread top with 1/2 cup whipped topping. Arrange whole strawberries over topping to within 1 inch of edge. Spread 1/2 cup topping on sides of torte. Decorate edge and top of torte with remaining whipped topping.

Silver Torte

Sugar
1 cup butter
2 cups flour, mixed with
1 teaspoon baking powder
1 tablespoon unflavored gelatin
8 eggs, separated

Juice and rind of 1 1/2 lemons
1/2 cup cream
Salt
1/2 package coconut
Rind of 1 orange

Mix 2 tablespoons sugar, butter and flour mixture together; place in 11"x 13" pan. Bake for 25 minutes at 350 degrees. Cool. Dissolve gelatin in 2/3 cup water. Set aside. Mix 1 cup sugar, beaten egg yolks, lemon juice and rind; cook until thickened. Add gelatin; cool. Beat egg whites until stiff; add 1 cup sugar and pinch of salt. Pour into custard mixture; let set. Spread custard mixture over cake. Beat cream; spread over custard. Mix coconut with orange rind. Sprinkle over whipped cream. Chill overnight. Yield: 12 servings.

Pineapple Torte

5 egg whites
3/4 teaspoon cream of tartar
2 cups sugar
1/2 cup chopped walnuts
2 cups unsalted cracker crumbs
2 packages Dream Whip
1 teaspoon vanilla
1 can pineapple pie filling
2 ripe bananas, diced (optional)

Beat egg whites until stiff enough to hold peaks. Add cream of tartar; beat until stiff. Fold in sugar, walnuts and cracker crumbs; spread into greased 9"x 13" baking pan. Bake for 25 minutes at 350 degrees. Remove from oven; cool. Whip Dream Whip according to package directions; add vanilla. Fold in pie filling and bananas; spread over baked torte. Refrigerate till served. Other flavors pie filling may be substituted for pineapple pie filling; grapes may be substituted for bananas. Yield: 12-15 servings.

Christmas Torte

6 eggs, separated
1 cup sugar
1 cup rusk crumbs
1/2 cup nutmeats
1 teaspoon vanilla
1 teaspoon baking powder
1 cup whipped topping
55 Milk Duds
1/2 cup milk
1/2 cup powdered sugar
2 tablespoons butter

Beat egg yolks with sugar; add crumbs, nutmeats, vanilla and baking powder. Fold in beaten egg whites. Pour into 9"x 13" pan. Bake for 30 minutes at 325 degrees. Cool. Cover with topping. Combine remaining ingredients; cook over medium heat until Milk Duds are melted. Drizzle over topping. Garnish each serving with additional whipped topping, red cherry and piece of citron for leaf. Yield: 12 servings.

Meringue Tarts

Sift 1 cup sugar, place on a platter; 3 egg whites, 1/2 teaspoon baking powder, 1/8 teaspoon salt. Combine in a small pitcher or cup: 1 teaspoon vanilla, 1 teaspoon vinegar, 1 teaspoon water. Whip the egg whites until they are stiff; add sifted sugar very slowly, 1/2 teaspoon at a time, alternating a few drops of the combined liquids. Beat constantly. When all the ingredients have been added, continue to beat for several minutes. Heap on lightly greased platter or dish from which it is to be served, (baking will not affect dish). Shape meringue like pie or tart with a heavy edge, using a spatula or knife. Bake in a very slow oven, 275 degrees for 1 hour or longer. When ready to serve, fill with sweetened fresh or stewed fruit, top with slightly sweetened and flavored whipped cream.

Also a good filling is this:

Prepare in double boiler: 4 beaten egg yolks, 1/2 cup sugar, juice and rind of 1 lemon, 1/2 cup water, 1 tablespoon flour. Stir and cook until thick; cool, whip 1 cup heavy cream. Fold in 1 teaspoon vanilla. Place layer of cream in meringue tart then the filling, then layer of cream. Chill for several hours. With electric beater, combine at high speed all ingredients except sugar; add gradually while beating. Serves six.

Pudding

1 quart bread crumbs
1 cup sweet milk
1 cup raisins
2 eggs
1 cup sugar
1 teaspoon each cloves, cinnamon, nutmeg and soda
2 teaspoons baking powder
4 teaspoons flour

Sift dry ingredients, add liquids, beaten together. Beat well and pour over bread crumbs, mixed with raisins. Steam about an hour in well-buttered pan. Test with straw. Serve with following sauce: 1 egg, 1 cup sugar (beaten together); boil 1/2 pint sweet milk, add lump of butter and a little vanilla. Pour over egg and sugar, cook until it thickens.

Pecan Tarts

3 ounces cream cheese,
   softened
1/2 cup butter, softened
1 cup sifted flour
2/3 cup broken pecans

1 egg
3/4 cup packed brown sugar
1 tablespoon vanilla extract
1/8 teaspoon salt

Blend cream cheese and 1/2 cup butter in mixing bowl. Add flour; mix well. Chill for 1 hour. Shape into 24 balls. Press over bottoms and sides of miniature muffin cups. Sprinkle pecans into tart shells. Combine egg, brown sugar, 1 tablespoon butter, vanilla and salt in mixer bowl; mix until smooth. Spoon into tart shells. Bake for 25 minutes or until set. Cool. The pastry for these tarts must be made ahead. Yield: 24 servings.

Liqueur Souffle

3 tablespoons flour
3/4 cup milk
1 tablespoon butter
2 tablespoons sugar
1/3 cup orange liqueur (curacao orange)
3 egg yolks
About 1/3 cup yellow cake, crumbled
10 egg whites
2 teaspoons cornstarch

Butter and sugar for a 2 quart ovenproof dish with straight sides (souffle dish). Confectioners' sugar to sprinkle over the souffle

Prepare batter as follows: measure flour into a non-aluminum pan. Add milk a little at a time, whisking constantly so that batter does not become lumpy. Let batter come to a boil, continuing to beat constantly. Let batter boil for 2 to 3 minutes. Beat vigorously the entire time. Add butter, sugar and half of the liqueur. Mix well. Remove pan from heat. Place it on a damp cloth so that it stands in place. Add egg yolks 1 at a time while batter is still hot. Beat vigorously the entire time. Let cake crumbs swell in remaining liqueur.

Hot Chocolate Souffle

Butter
Sugar
3/4 cup chocolate chips
4 egg yolks

1 cup confectioners' sugar, sifted
5 egg whites, room temperature
1/2 teaspoon cream of tartar

Grease 6 inch souffle dish generously with butter; coat inside with sugar, shaking out excess. Combine 2 tablespoons cold water and chocolate chips in top of double boiler. Place over hot water until chocolate chips are melted; beat with wire whisk until blended. Cut 2 tablespoons butter into small pieces; add to chocolate 1 piece at a time, beating until butter is melted. Cool slightly. Place egg yolks in large mixer bowl; beat with electric mixer until lemon-colored. Add confectioners' sugar gradually; beat until thick. Add 1/4 of chocolate mixture; beat with wire whisk until blended. Add remaining chocolate mixture; beat until well mixed. Beat egg whites and cream of tartar with electric mixer until stiff peaks form. Fold 1/4 of egg whites into chocolate mixture; blend well. Gently fold in remaining egg whites until well mixed. Spoon into prepared souffle dish; smooth top. Bake in preheated 400 degree oven for 35 minutes or until set. Dust with additional confectioners' sugar, if desired, serve immediately. Yield: 6 servings.

Cranberry Tart Cake

2 1/2 cups sifted flour
1 cup sugar
1 teaspoon soda
1 teaspoon baking powder
1/4 teaspoon salt
Grated rind of 2 oranges
1 cup broken English walnuts

1 cup chopped dates
1 cup chopped cranberries
2 eggs, beaten
1 cup buttermilk
3/4 cup oil
1 cup orange juice
1 cup sugar

Combine flour, 1 cup sugar, soda, baking powder, salt and orange rind in bowl. Mix in walnuts, dates and cranberries. Blend eggs, buttermilk and oil in bowl until smooth. Add to cranberry mixture; stir until well mixed. Spoon into greased and floured cake pan. Bake in tube pan at 350 degrees for 1 hour. Cool to lukewarm in pan. Heat orange juice and 1 cup sugar in saucepan until sugar is dissolved. Remove cake to serving plate. Pour glaze over cake very gradually, allowing cake to absorb mixture. Cool completely. Refrigerate, wrapped in foil, for 24 hours before serving. This holiday cake must be made ahead and freezes well. For ease of preparation, buy sugared chopped dates and chop cranberries in blender. Yield: 12 servings.

Easy Chocolate Mousse

1 very large Hershey bar with almonds	1 1/2 cup chocolate, chocolate chip cookie (yes) crumbs
1 (12 ounce) container Cool Whip	6 tablespoons butter
1/4 cup Kahlua	Toasted, sliced almonds

Blend cookie crumbs and butter to make a crumb crust. Pat into bottoms of 6 to 8 parfait, or, if preferred, champagne glasses. Melt Hershey bar and mix with Cool Whip and Kahlua. Pour into the prepared glasses and sprinkle with toasted, sliced almonds. Freeze until serving time. To serve, remove from freezer, garnish with a dollop of whipped cream, and chocolate curls, if desired. This dessert may be made a day ahead. It is very rich; do not make large portions. Note: Any favorite cookie may be used for crumb crust.

Easy Apricot Mousse

Boil 1 pint water with 1 cup sugar until you have 1 cup syrup, not too thick. Put 1 quart can apricots, through sieve, removing skins. Add apricot juice from apricots, and juice from 1/2 lemon to syrup. Cool and half freeze. Add 1 cup canned milk or cream and stir thorough the half frozen mixture, then freeze hard. Canned peaches or canned pineapple may be used instead of apricots. Canned milk does just as well as cream in this recipe.

Pie with Pineapple Mousse

Crust 1 1/4 cups flour	1/4 cup sugar
1/4 cup sugar	3/4 cup whipping cream
7 tablespoons margarine or butter	3 1/2 ounces cooking chocolate
1/3 cup cottage cheese	Mousse
2 envelopes gelatin	1 (18 ounce) can pineapple
3 eggs, separated	slices in juice

Measure flour and sugar into a bowl. Crumble margarine into the mixture. Add cottage cheese, and make into a workable dough. (You can also place all the ingredients in a food processor and mix into a dough.) Refrigerate 1 hour. Pour juice from pineapple can (about 3/4

(continued)

cup) into a pot. Add gelatin and let it soak in the juice for about 5 minutes, until soft. Then melt gelatin in the juice over low heat. Separate egg yolks and whites. Beat yolks together with the sugar. Beat egg whites into stiff peaks. Whip cream. Cut pineapple slices into pieces; save 3 to 4 slices for decoration. Mix egg yolk mixture, whipped cream and pieces of pineapple together. Add juice in an even, little trickle while stirring constantly. Mix well. Fold in egg whites. Refrigerate mousse for about 1 hour so that it becomes partially firm. Preheat oven to 400 degrees. Press dough into a pie plate or ovenproof dish. Prick well. Bake pie crust for about 20 minutes in the oven. Meanwhile, melt about 3 ounces of cooking chocolate over very low heat. Remove pie crust from oven. Spread chocolate in the crust. Allow crust to become cold. When mousse has become partially firm, spread it over chocolate in the pie crust. Place dessert back in refrigerator to become totally firm. Decorate with slices of pineapple and chopped chocolate. Yield: 1 - 9" pie.

Apricot Souffle

1 package dried apricots
1/2 cup scalded almonds
(Pistachio almonds should preferably be used but they are very difficult to find.)
3/4 to 1 1/4 cups sugar
4 egg whites
Butter for greasing the pan

Thoroughly rinse apricots. Place them to soak for awhile in water. Then boil apricots in water until they become soft.

Finely chop almonds. Strain apricots. Mix them with sugar and almonds. Beat egg whites into as stiff peaks as possible. Fold half of the whites into the apricot puree. Fold in rest of egg whites with a few large, deep turns of a spoon. Pour batter into a generously greased souffle form and bake in 400 degree oven for about 30 minutes. Remove souffle from oven. Garnish with a few extra chopped almonds. Serve immediately, preferably with softly whipped cream that has been flavored with brandy. If you pour batter into individual souffle dishes, baking time should be decreased to about 20 minutes. Yield: 4 servings.

Basic Dessert Crepe Batter

4 eggs	1 cup milk
1 cup flour	1/4 cup water
2 tablespoons sugar	1 tablespoon melted butter, cooled

Mixer or whisk method: beat eggs in medium mixing bowl. Gradually add flour and sugar alternately with milk and water, beating until smooth. Beat in melted butter.

Blender or food processor method: combine ingredients in container; blend about 1 minute. Scrape down sides with rubber spatula: blend 15 seconds or until smooth. Refrigerate batter at least 1 hour before use.

Butter or oil a crepe pan and heat pan over moderate heat. Pour a little batter in corner of pan. Shake pan gently until batter completely covers bottom. Cook for 1 minute. Turn crepe over with spatula and cook briefly. Pile crepes on plate with a little sugar sprinkled between each crepe. Yield: 20-25 crepes.

Mixed Fruit Crepes with Whipped Cream

3 bananas	1 pound fesh or canned peaches
2 tablespoons heavy cream	
1 tablespoon sugar	1 pound fresh or canned pears
12 dessert crepes	2 tablespoons butter
(see basic dessert crepe batter)	

Mash bananas with cream and sugar; cover surface of each crepe. Cut peaches and pears into small pieces; lay over bananas. Roll or fold crepes; place in buttered ovenproof dish. Dot with butter. Bake in preheated 400 degree oven for 15 minutes. Serve with whipped cream. Yield: 6 servings.

Strawberry Cream Crepes

4 cups fresh strawberries,
  sliced
2 tablespoons sugar
1 (14 ounce) can
  sweetened condensed milk
1/4 cup lemon juice

1/2 cup heavy cream, whipped
12 dessert crepes
  (see basic dessert crepe batter)
Whipped cream for garnish
12 whole strawberries for
  garnish

Sprinkle sliced strawberries with sugar, set aside. Beat milk with lemon juice until thick. Fold in strawberries and whipped cream. Divide among crepes; fold. Garnish with additional whipped cream and a strawberry centered on cream. Yield: 6 servings.

Hot Ice Cream Crepes

1 pint coffee ice cream
12 cold dessert crepes (see basic dessert crepe batter)
Chocolate sauce

Preheat oven to 475 degrees. Divide ice cream among crepes; roll up. Place in ovenproof dish. Bake in hot oven about 2 to 3 minutes. Serve with cold chocolate sauce. Yield: 4 servings.

Peach Cream Parfait

1 1/2 cups cottage cheese
1/2 teaspoon almond extract
1/2 teaspoon salt
2 tablespoons sugar
1 cup cream, whipped
1 1/2 cups to 2 cups (1 pound) peaches, sweetened, sliced
Slivered Almonds

Beat cottage cheese until smooth. Add extract, salt, sugar and mix well. Fold in whipped cream. Alternate layers of cottage cheese mix and cut peaches in parfait glasses. End and begin with cheese. Top with almonds. Chill well before serving.

Peach and Pudding Parfait

1 (3 5/8 ounce) package vanilla pudding and pie filling mix
1 1/2 cups milk
1/2 cup commercial sour cream
2 cups fresh or canned diced peaches

Combine vanilla pudding and milk in saucepan; cook over medium heat, stirring constantly, until mixture reaches boiling point. Remove from heat and stir in sour cream. Cool thoroughly, stirring frequently. Chill. When ready to serve, alternate layers of pudding and peaches in parfait glasses. Yield: 6 servings.

Vanilla Grape Parfaits

Here's a recipe with regal colors that is simply scrumptious.
3 cups nonfat vanilla frozen yogurt, softened
1 can (6 ounce) unsweetened frozen grape juice concentrate,
    slightly thawed
1/2 cup Low Fat Whipped Topping
Red grapes (garnish)

Place 1 cup of the yogurt into the bottom of each of 6 parfait glasses. Spoon some of the grape juice over the yogurt, reserving some for another layer. Cover the grape juice with the remaining yogurt. Top with the remaining grape juice. Freeze for 1 hour.
When ready to serve, top each parfait with the whipped topping. Garnish with the grapes. Yield: 6 servings.

Raspberry Peach Tapioca Parfaits

Here's a perfectly peachy way to boost your intake of calcium: each serving has 160 milligrams of the bone-strengthening mineral.
1 cup basic tapioca pudding   1/2 cup fresh raspberry sauce
1/2 cup fresh peach sauce   Fresh raspberries (garnish)

Place 1/4 cup of the pudding into the bottom of each of 4 parfait glasses. Top each with 2 tablespoons of the raspberry sauce. Divide the remaining tapioca among the glasses. Spoon 2 tablespoons of the peach sauce on each. Top with the raspberries. Yield: 4 servings.

Strawberry Rhubarb Pudding Parfaits

All the terrific strawberry rhubarb pie flavor minus the fat-rich crust. What a great way to get a wholesome serving of calcium, potassium and vitamin C!

2 1/2 cup skim milk	1 cup strawberries, sliced
1/3 cup quick cooking	2 tablespoons water
long grain rice	1 tablespoon cornstarch
1/3 cup sugar	Strawberries or mint sprigs
1/2 pound fresh or frozen	(garnish)
rhubarb, cut into 1/2 inch pieces	

Combine the milk, rice and 5 teaspoons of the sugar in a heavy 4 quart saucepan. Bring to a boil over medium high heat. Reduce the heat to low; cover and simmer, stirring occasionally, until the rice is very tender and the mixture is creamy, about 10 minutes. Remove the saucepan from the heat; cool. Meanwhile, combine the rhubarb, strawberries, water, cornstarch and the remaining 1/4 cup of sugar in a medium saucepan; bring to a boil over medium heat. Reduce the heat to low; cover and cook, stirring occasionally, until the rhubarb is tender, about 10 minutes. Remove from the heat; cool. Into each of 4 parfait glasses or 8 ounce wine goblets, spoon 3 tablespoons of the strawberry rhubarb mixture. Top with 1/2 cup of the rice pudding mixture, then 2 tablespoons of strawberry rhubarb mixture. Garnish with small strawberries or mint sprigs. Yield: 4 servings.

Melon, Berries and Sherbet Parfaits

Relax in the shade with luscious fruit and icy sherbet. And it's okay to indulge; this one's high in vitamin C and low in calories.

2 cantaloupes, honeydew, melons or watermelons
1 pint lemon or orange sherbet
1 pint fresh blueberries or raspberries
Mint leaves (garnish)
Low Fat Whipped Topping (garnish)

Using a melon baller, scoop out small balls of melon and chill. Using the same baller, scoop out small balls of sherbet, dividing them among 8 parfait glasses and alternating them with the melon balls and berries. Garnish with the mint leaves and whipped topping. Serve immediately. Yield: 8 servings.

Toasted Almond Parfaits

1 1/4 cup skim milk
1 package (3 1/2 ounces) vanilla instant pudding
1/2 teaspoon almond extract
1/2 cup evaporated skim milk
1 tablespoon confectioners' sugar
2 peaches, coarsely chopped
1 tablespoon sliced almonds, toasted
Low Fat Whipped Topping (garnish)
Toasted almonds (garnish)

Using only the 1 1/4 cups of skim milk, prepare the pudding in a medium bowl according to the manufacturer's directions. Beat in the almond extract. Set aside. In another bowl, beat the evaporated skim milk and confectioners' sugar with an electric mixer at high speed until soft peaks form, fold the whipped milk into the pudding mixture. Into each of 4 parfait glasses, spoon 3/4 cup of the pudding mixture; top with 2 tablespoons of chopped peaches and 3/4 teaspoon of toasted almonds. Repeat layering. Garnish each parfait with a dollop of the whipped topping and a sprinkling of toasted almonds. Yield: 4 servings.

Apricot Parfaits

Here's a unique cheese parfait that's short on prep time and long on fruity apricot flavor.
16 ounces part skim ricotta cheese
1/4 cup pineapple juice concentrate, thawed
1 tablespoon honey
1/2 teaspoon almond extract
1 can (16 ounces) apricot halves, packed in juice
2 tablespoons toasted shredded coconut

In a blender or food processor, process the ricotta, juice concentrate, honey and almond extract until very smooth and creamy. Drain the apricot halves and cut each into 2 or 3 pieces. Spoon a few tablespoons of the ricotta mixture into the bottoms of 4 parfait glasses. Top with a few apricot pieces. Continue to layer until the ricotta cheese and apricots have been used. Sprinkle with the coconut. Serve immediately or chill. Yield: 4 servings.

Cantaloupe Cake

3/4 cup oil
1 3/4 cups sugar
3 eggs
2 cups self-rising flour
1 teaspoon cinnamon
1 teaspoon baking soda
1 cup fresh cantaloupe, diced
1 cup fresh apples, diced
1 cup white raisins

Combine oil, sugar and eggs; beat until smooth. Add flour, cinnamon and baking soda; mix until smooth. Fold in cantaloupe, apple and raisins. Spread mixture into a greased 9"x 13" pan. Bake in a 375 degree oven for 20 minutes. Lower temperature to 325 degrees and bake 10 more minutes; cool and frost.

Frosting:
Frost with 7 1/2 ounce box of Jiffy Frosting Mix. Add 1/2 teaspoon vanilla to the prepared mix. (Follow directions according to box.)

Christmas Lane Cake

3 1/4 cups flour
3 1/2 teaspoons baking powder
1/2 teaspoon salt
1 cup butter or margarine
2 cups sugar
1 cup milk
8 egg whites

Sift dry ingredients. Cream butter and sugar until light and fluffy; add vanilla. Add alternately dry ingredients with milk. Beat egg whites until stiff but not dry, and fold into batter. Put into 4 greased and floured 9 inch layer cake pans. Bake at 375 degrees for 15 to 20 minutes, or until tested done. Remove from pans and cool.

(continued)

Christmas Lane Filling

8 egg yolks
1 1/4 cups sugar
1 1/2 cups butter
1 cup chopped pecans
1 cup grated coconut
1 cup chopped candied cherries
1/3 cup cooking wine (optional)

Place egg yolks in saucepan and beat slightly, mix in sugar and butter and cook over low heat, stirring constantly until it begins to thicken. Remove from heat, add rest of ingredients and cool. Spread between layers of cake.

Christmas Lane Frosting

1 1/3 cups dark corn syrup
Dash of salt
2 egg whites
1 teaspoon vanilla

In small saucepan, heat syrup until boiling. Beat egg whites, add salt and slowly pour in syrup while continuing to beat until frosting is fluffy and forms peaks. Fold in vanilla. Spread over cake top and sides. Sprinkle with coconut, if desired.

Tomato Soup Cake

1/2 cup butter
1 cup sugar
1 (10 ounce) can tomato soup
1/2 cup walnuts
1/2 cup mixed cherries
1 1/2 cup flour
2 teaspoons (scant) baking powder
1/2 teaspoon each nutmeg, cinnamon and cloves

Mix first 3 ingredients; heat until butter melts. Add walnuts and cherries. Mix dry ingredients together. Mix all ingredients together. Bake at 300 degrees for 40 to 45 minutes. Yield: 24 servings.

Raspberry Coffee Cake

1 (3 ounce) package cream cheese, softened
2 tablespoons butter or margarine, softened
2 cups biscuit mix
1/3 cup milk
1/2 cup raspberry preserves (or apricot)

Cut cream cheese and butter into biscuit mix with a pastry blender until mixture resembles coarse meal. Add milk, stirring with a fork until dry ingredients are moistened. Turn dough out onto a well-floured surface, and knead 10 times. Roll dough into a 12"x18" inch rectangle on waxed paper. Spread preserves over rectangle, leaving a 1/2 inch margin around edges; carefully fold each side to center of dough. Firmly pinch ends to seal. Transfer dough to a greased baking sheet.

Using kitchen shears, make 1 1/2 inch cuts about one inch apart along each side of coffee cake, cutting one-third of the way through dough at each cut. Bake at 400 degrees for 20 to 25 minutes. Pour glaze over coffee cake while still warm.

Glaze:

1 cup sifted powdered sugar
2 tablespoons milk
1/2 teaspoon vanilla
Combine all ingredients, mixing well.

Dark Fruit Cake

1 pound each raisins, pitted	12 eggs
dates, citron, currants	4 cups sifted flour
1 1/2 pounds candied cherries	1 teaspoon soda
1/2 pound candied orange peel	1/2 teaspoon each nutmeg,
1/4 pound candied lemon peel	mace, cloves
1 1/2 pounds shelled nuts	1 teaspoon each cinnamon,
1 pound butter	allspice, salt
1 pound light brown sugar	1 cup molasses

Cut fruit into small pieces and break nuts. Cream butter and sugar together. Beat eggs and add to cream mixture. Blend well. Sift dry ingredients together and add to creamed mixture alternately with molasses. Add batter to fruits and nuts. Mix together thoroughly, using hands if necessary. Pour into two large tube pans which have been greased and lined with greased brown paper cut to fit. Cover tops with aluminum foil squeezed tightly down around the edge of pan. Bake at 275 degrees until done, (about 4 hours and 20 minutes). Test the cakes with a toothpick to determine doneness as ovens and pans will make the time vary. Remove the foil the last 30 minutes or so to allow tops of cakes to dry out. Makes 2 cakes or about 15 pounds.

Fresh Apple Cake with Topping

1 1/2 cups vegetable oil	1 teaspoon each soda,
2 cups sugar	salt, cinnamon
3 cups flour	1 teaspoon vanilla
3 eggs	3 cups fresh apples, chopped
1 cup nuts	

Blend vegetable oil, sugar and eggs well. Sift flour, soda, salt and cinnamon together. Add to sugar mixture at intervals. Add vanilla. Peel and chop apples and add at once to prevent browning. Bake in a greased tube pan for 1 hour and 15 minutes at 350 degrees.

Topping:

1 1/2 cups brown sugar	1 cup evaporated milk
1/2 cup butter	

Cook until fairly thick and pour over cake.

Pecan Slices

1/2 cup margarine	1/2 cup flaked coconut
1/4 cup sugar	1 cup chopped pecans
1 egg	2 tablespoons flour
1 1/4 cups sifted flour	1/2 teaspoon baking powder
1/8 teaspoon salt	1/2 teaspoon salt
1/2 teaspoon vanilla	1 teaspoon vanilla
2 eggs, beaten	1 1/2 cups confectioners' sugar
1 1/2 cups brown sugar	Lemon juice

Cream sugar and margarine. Beat in one egg. Combine flour and salt; add in three parts to creamed mixture; blend well. Work in vanilla. Pat dough evenly in a 9"x 12" pan. Combine egg, brown sugar, coconut, pecans, flour, baking powder, salt, vanilla and spread over the dough. Bake for 25 minutes at 350 degrees. When cool, ice with sugar thinned to a spreading consistency with lemon juice. Cut into bars.
Yield: 3 dozen bars.

Strawberry Short Cake

1 cup flour	1 tablespoon butter
2 teaspoons baking powder	2 cups sliced strawberries
1/4 teaspoon salt	1/2 cup sugar
1 teaspoon sugar	1 cup cream, whipped
1/2 cup milk	

Sift dry ingredients and cut in butter. Add milk to make dough. Roll thin, cut in 3 inch circles and bake on cookie sheet. Bake 450 degrees for 10 to 12 minutes. Heat strawberries and sugar until sugar dissolves. Spread between pastry and top with whipped cream.

Butternut Cake

2 cups sugar	2 1/2 cups cake flour
1 cup shortening	1 cup milk
4 eggs	1 tablespoon butternut flavoring
1/2 cup self-rising flour	Pinch of salt

Cream sugar and shortening on high until very smooth. Add eggs one at a time. Add flour and milk alternately. Add flavoring and salt. Turn into greased and floured tube pan and bake at 325 degrees for 1 hour.

Mound Cake

2/3 cup margarine
1 1/2 cups sugar
2 eggs
2 cups plain flour, sifted
1/2 teaspoon soda
1 1/4 teaspoons baking powder
4 tablespoons cocoa
1 cup buttermilk

Cream together margarine and sugar. Add eggs, blend well. Sift together flour, soda, baking powder, cocoa. Alternately add flour mixture and buttermilk. Place in 2, 9" greased and floured cake pans. Bake 350 degrees for 25 minutes. Cool. Split the two layers to make 4 layers.

Fudge Frosting

1/3 cup milk
1/4 cup margarine
1 (6 ounce) package semisweet chocolate morsels
1 teaspoon vanilla
2 1/4 cups confectioners' sugar, sifted

Place all ingredients in a saucepan. Boil together for 5 minutes. This goes between each layer.

Coconut Filling

1 cup evaporated milk
2 cups coconut
12 large marshmallows
1 cup sugar
1 cup chopped pecans

Combine milk and margarine. Bring to a boil and cook for 5 minutes. Remove from heat and add chocolate, vanilla and sugar. Blend together well. Frost cake.

Hawaiian Pineapple Nut Cake

1 (8 ounce) can crushed
 pineapple, drained
1/2 cup chopped nuts
2 eggs, beaten
1/2 cup melted butter

3/4 cup flour
1/4 teaspoon baking soda
1 teaspoon salt
1 cup sugar
1 cup sweetened whipped
 cream

Sift together flour, soda and salt. Combine butter and sugar. Add eggs and mix well. Sift flour mixture into the batter, stirring until blended. Add pineapple and nuts. Pour into greased 9" pan. Bake for 1 hour at 325 degrees. Top with whipped cream for serving. Yield: serves 6-8.

Walnut Chocolate Cake

1 cup water
1 1/2 teaspoons soda
1/2 cup cocoa
2/3 cup butter
1 3/4 cups sugar

2 eggs
2 1/2 cups sifted flour
1/2 teaspoon salt
1 teaspoon vanilla
3/4 cup buttermilk
1 cup chopped walnuts

Filling:

2 cups sugar
2 squares chocolate

1/2 cup milk
1 stick butter

Mix water, soda and cocoa and let stand while mixing batter. Cream sugar and butter. Add eggs, one at a time. Add alternately flour, salt and buttermilk. Combine batter with first mixture. Add walnuts. Bake at 350 degrees for 30-40 minutes in three 8" layer pans.

Filling Bring to a boil and cook 2 minutes without stirring. Beat well and spread. Yield: 20 slices.

Maraschino Cherry Cake

2 teaspoons baking powder
2 cups sifted flour
1/4 teaspoon salt
1/3 cup butter or shortening
1 cup sugar
2 eggs, well beaten

2/3 cup milk
1/2 teaspoon vanilla
1/2 cup nutmeats,
  finely broken
16 maraschino cherries,
  cut into eighths

Sift baking powder, flour and salt three times. Cream shortening thoroughly; add sugar gradually, creaming until light and fluffy. Add eggs; add flour mixture alternately with milk, beating after each addition until smooth. Add vanilla. Pour into greased pan. Sprinkle nutmeats and cherries over top. Bake at 350 degrees for 1 hour or until done.

Walnut Cream Cookies

3 tablespoons butter
3 tablespoons cream cheese
6 tablespoons powdered sugar
2 egg yolks, beaten

1 teaspoon vanilla
1/4 teaspoon lemon extract
1 cup sifted flour
1/2 cup chopped black walnuts

Thoroughly cream butter, cheese and sugar; add egg yolks and flavorings. Beat well. Add flour; then add nuts. Drop by teaspoonfuls onto ungreased cookie sheet. Bake at 350 degrees for 15 minutes. Yield: 3 dozen.

Lace Wafers

1/2 cup butter or margarine
2/3 cup sugar
2 eggs
2 teaspoons vanilla

1/2 cup finely chopped nuts
1/3 cup flour
1/2 teaspoon salt

Cream butter with sugar until fluffy; beat in eggs and vanilla. Stir in nuts, flour and salt just until blended. Drop from teaspoon 4 inches apart on well-buttered cookie sheet. Bake, several at a time, at 350 degrees for 7 minutes. Loosen each cookie with spatula immediately. Cool on rack. Yield: 5 dozen.

No Bake Chocolate Cookies

1 stick butter or margarine	1/2 cup peanut butter
1/2 cup milk	1 teaspoon vanilla extract
1/2 cup cocoa	2 1/2 cups oatmeal
2 cups sugar	

Combine margarine, milk, cocoa and sugar in saucepan; bring to a rolling boil. Continue boiling for 3 minutes. Remove from heat; add peanut butter, vanilla and oatmeal. Stir well until thoroughly mixed and slightly cooled. Drop by spoonfuls onto waxed paper. Cool. Yield: 2 dozen.

Chocolate Nut Clusters

3 squares unsweetened chocolate	1 cup sugar
1 cup sifted all-purpose flour	2 eggs
3/4 teaspoon salt	2 teaspoons vanilla
1/2 teaspoon baking powder	3 cups coarsely broken
1/2 cup margarine or butter	English walnuts

Melt chocolate over very low heat; set aside. Sift together flour, salt and baking powder. Cream margarine with sugar until fluffy. Add 1 unbeaten egg; mix thoroughly then add other egg. Beat well. Add vanilla and melted chocolate. Stir in flour and nuts. Drop by teaspoonfuls on greased cookie sheet. Bake in moderate oven, 350 degrees, just 10 minutes. Cookies should not brown during baking. Cool in rack. Yield: 40 (2 inch) cookies.

Pineapple Cookies

1 1/2 cup sugar	1/2 teaspoon soda
1/2 cup Crisco	1 tablespoon baking powder
2 eggs	Pinch of salt
1 cup crushed pineapple	1 cup chopped nuts
3 1/2 cups flour	1 cup raisins

Cream sugar, Crisco and eggs. Add remaining ingredients. Drop on cookie sheet from teaspoon. Bake for 15 minutes at 375 degrees. Yield: 3 dozen cookies.

Gina's Butter Cookies

1/2 pound butter	2 1/4 cups flour
1/2 cup sugar	1/2 teaspoon baking powder
1 egg	1 teaspoon vanilla

Cream butter, sugar and egg until fluffy. Sift baking powder with flour; add small amount at a time to butter mixture. Lastly, add vanilla and mix well. Use cookie press for desired shapes. Bake on greased (lightly) cookie sheet in 350 degrees oven for 10-12 minutes or until brown. These may be garnished with nuts or candied fruits before baking, if desired. These are delicious and keep well. Note: Do not add milk or any other liquid to batter, this will make cookies tough.

Potato Chip Cookies

1 cup minus	2 cups flour
2 tablespoons shortening	1 teaspoon soda
1 cup sugar	1/2 teaspoon salt
1 cup brown sugar	2 cups crushed potato chips
2 eggs	Chopped nuts (optional)
1 teaspoon vanilla	

Cream shortening and sugars; add eggs and vanilla. Sift flour with soda and salt. Blend dry ingredients with creamed mixture. Add potato chips and nuts. Chill; roll into walnut-sized balls. Press down with fork. Bake at 325 degrees for 10 minutes. Yield: 4 dozen cookies.

MeMa's Cookies

1 cup butter	2 cups nutmeats
2 cups light brown sugar	(pecans especially good)
2 eggs	1 teaspoon baking powder
1 cup cold coffee	1 teaspoon soda
2 cups raisins	1 teaspoon cinnamon
3 cups flour	1 teaspoon vanilla

Add more flour if necessary. Drop cookies onto lightly greased cookie sheet. Bake in 350 degree oven for approximately 10 minutes.

Graham Crispies

18 (2 1/2 inch long)	1 cup firmly packed
graham crackers, halved	dark brown sugar
1 cup butter or margarine	1 cup chopped nuts

Line cookie sheet with aluminum foil. Cover with graham crackers.
Melt butter in saucepan; stir in brown sugar. Bring mixture to a boil and
boil 2 minutes. Sprinkle nuts over crackers. Pour sauce over nuts and
bake at 375 degrees for 10 minutes. Break crackers apart before they
cool. Yield: about 3 dozen.
Coconut: Add 1 cup coconut to cookie batter.
Raisin Spice: Add 1 teaspoon ground cinnamon and 1/4 teaspoon
ground nutmeg with dry ingredients. Omit vanilla. Add 1 cup raisins to
cookie batter.

Cherries A La Mode

3 tablespoons lemon juice	1 (21 ounce) can cherry
2 tablespoons brown sugar	pie filling
1/8 teaspoon salt	Commercial pound cake
	1 quart chocolate ice cream

Combine lemon juice, sugar, salt and pie filling in a 1 quart
saucepan; heat 5 minutes. Spoon sauce over pound cake slices, add
scoop of ice cream and top with additional cherry sauce. Serve
immediately. Yield: 6 to 9 servings.

Cranberry Crumble

1 (16 ounce) can whole	1/2 cup firmly packed
cranberry sauce	brown sugar
1/2 cup quick-cooking oats,	1/4 cup butter or margarine
uncooked	Whipped cream or
1/4 cup all-purpose flour	vanilla ice cream

Spread cranberry sauce in a 9" pie pan. Combine oats, flour and
brown sugar; cut in butter until crumbly. Sprinkle over cranberries. Bake
at 350 degrees for 25 minutes. Top with whipped cream or vanilla ice
cream. Yield: 5 to 6 servings.

Master Oatmeal Cookies

1 cup all-purpose flour	2 eggs
1 teaspoon baking powder	1 teaspoon vanilla extract
1/2 teaspoon salt	1/3 cup milk
3/4 cup shortening	3 cups quick-cooking
(room temperature)	oats, uncooked
1 cup firmly packed brown sugar	

Combine flour, baking powder and salt. Add shortening, sugar, eggs, vanilla and about half the milk. Beat until smooth, about 2 minutes. Stir in remaining milk and oats. Drop from a teaspoon onto greased baking sheet and bake at 375 degrees for 12-15 minutes. Yield: 4 dozen cookies.

Chocolate Mint Delights

2 cups vanilla wafer crumbs	4 eggs
1 cup real butter	2 teaspoons vanilla
1 box powdered sugar	1 teaspoon peppermint
4 squares melted	flavoring
unsweetened chocolate	

Crush and roll enough vanilla wafers to make 2 cups. Divide half of resulting crumbs among 20 cupcake papers and set aside. Beat butter, sugar and chocolate very well. Add 4 eggs and beat again, very well. Add 2 teaspoons vanilla and 1 teaspoon peppermint flavoring and beat thoroughly. Pour chocolate mixture in prepared cupcake papers and top with remaining crumbs. Freeze. These keep for months in freezer if they are well wrapped. Serve directly from freezer with a dollop of whipped cream on top. Yield: 18 to 20 servings.

Pfeffernusse Cookies (German)

2 cups sugar	1 teaspoon cinnamon
1 cup shortening	1 1/2 tablespoon anise seed
2 eggs	1/2 teaspoon allspice
2 cups white Karo syrup	1/2 teaspoon salt
1 cup buttermilk	9 or more cups flour
1 1/2 teaspoon soda	

Mix all ingredients well. Set in cool place overnight. Make small balls the size of a thimble and flatten out. Bake 15 to 20 minutes at 375 degrees.

Snickerdoodles

1/2 cup soft shortening	2 teaspoons cream of tartar
1/2 cup melted margarine	1 teaspoon baking soda
1 1/2 cups sugar	4 tablespoons sugar
2 eggs	4 teaspoons cinnamon
2 3/4 cup flour	

Mix first four ingredients thoroughly. Sift together flour, cream of tartar and soda, and stir into first mixture. Form into balls the size of walnuts, and roll in mixture of the sugar and cinnamon. Place 2 inches apart on ungreased baking sheet. Bake in 400 degree oven for 10 minutes.

Dutch Lace Cookies

1 pound light brown sugar	2 cups flour
1/2 cup plus 2 tablespoons water	1 full teaspoon cinnamon
1/2 pound margarine, creamed	1/2 pound sliced almonds

Mix sugar and water. Add creamed margarine, followed by flour, cinnamon and almonds. Mix well and drop by small spoonfuls, far apart, as these spread out. Bake in 350 degree oven for 10-12 minutes, until crisp around edges. Let cool on cookie sheet for a couple of minutes before removing to cooling rack. Store in airtight "Christmas" tins.

Tea for Two

There's tea I've made for you and me,
I'm asking on my knees,
Please come to share with me, O Lord,
for I hope you will be pleased.
My gates are not made of pearls
and my roads not made of gold,
but one day Lord I'll join you up there,
for the Bible says, I'm told,
Until I do please join me,
for I've made tea for two,
I've made one for me, O Lord,
and the other is for you.

Gina Palmer

Notes

Favorite Tea Recipes

Favorite Recipes

Reorder Additional Copies

Mail to:

(SOUTHERN STYLE) *Tea Time*

did someone say tea?

204 East Bay Street   Savannah, GA 31401

Please mail _____ copy(ies) of your teabook   @ $12.95 each _____
    Postage and Packaging   @ $2.50 each _____
    Georgia residents please add 6% sales tax   @   .96 each _____

Mail books to:

    Name _____

    Address _____

    City, State, Zip _____

Published by Rosemary Arrington Newman and Sharon Arrington Strickland
Printed by Allied Printing   *First Edition*

- -

Reorder Additional Copies

Mail to:

(SOUTHERN STYLE) *Tea Time*

did someone say tea?

204 East Bay Street   Savannah, GA 31401

Please mail _____ copy(ies) of your teabook   @ $12.95 each _____
    Postage and Packaging   @ $2.50 each _____
    Georgia residents please add 6% sales tax   @   .96 each _____

Mail books to:

    Name _____

    Address _____

    City, State, Zip _____

Published by Rosemary Arrington Newman and Sharon Arrington Strickland
Printed by Allied Printing   *First Edition*

INDEX

INDEX